《文部科学省後援》

技術英検
1級問題集

一般社団法人日本能率協会
JSTC技術英語委員会

技術英検 1 級（2020～2023）&【旧検定名称】工業英検準2級（2019）過去15回分収録

2024
年度版

JN098148

日本能率協会マネジメントセンター

技術英語とは

　「技術英語」と聞くと、どのような内容の英語を想像するでしょうか。「難しい科学の文章が出るに違いない」、「学校の英語の授業で習った英単語だけでは合格できない」、「理系の人たち専用の試験」といったことではないでしょうか。しかし、そんなことはまったくありません。

　技術英語にあたる英語は "Technical Communication (in English)"、また、ライティングのみを示すのであれば "Technical Writing (in English)" です。つまり、この「技術」というのは、科学のジャンルの１つである「テクノロジー」ではなく、「テクニカル・コミュニケーション」という「英語でのコミュニケーションの手法」がベースであるということを意味しています。

　テクニカル・コミュニケーションについては、米国でもさまざまな定義があります。最新の定義をうまくまとめてある "Introduction to Technical and Professional Communication"（Brigitte Mussack 著）の定義を引用すると、「テクニカル・コミュニケーションは技術の説明に加え、専門的な内容を分かりやすく説明すること、読み手に行って欲しい内容を説明すること、ものの定義、指示、情報の提供、説得」と書かれています。そして「内容だけではなく、書き方も重要である」と追記しています。このような特徴があるために、論理的な物事の説明に向いているわけです。

　テクニカル・コミュニケーションはもともと、装置やシステムの仕組みやマニュアルを説明するための手法として始まりました。しかし、今では業界や業種を超え、多くの企業や大学で推奨されています。異なる名称が付けられていることもありますが、テクニカル・コミュニケーションが提唱している３Ｃ（Clear, Concise, Correct）、そしてパラグラフ・ライティングと内容は変わりません。「物事を分かりやすく、正確に伝える」ということを追求していくと、自然とコミュニケーションの究極の形である３Ｃとパラグラフに辿り着くということでしょう。

　本検定の各級に共通しているのは、英語力（テクニカル・コミュニケーションの力）があれば、理系、文系を問わず、どのようなバックグラウンドの方でも合格できる、という点です。科学の知識は必要とせず、あくまでも英語力が問われる試験となるように問題を作成しています。どの級も、常に最新で、読んでも面白い、一般的な科学、ビジネス分野から出題されます。各級を順番に合格していくことで、一般的な意味での英語力向上に加え、せっかく向上した英語力をどう有効的に使うか、という力も正しい順序で高めていくことができます。本検定の内容は、英語を実践的に使う際に大いに役立つでしょう。

　技術情報の交流や輸出入が増えている現在、コミュニケーションの手段として、技術英語の正しい理解と活用が学界、産業界で必須のものとなっています。ぜひ本検定を通して、世界基準の英語力を身につけていただきたいと願っています。

〈工業英検から技術英検へ〉

　本検定の事業母体であった公益社団法人技術英語協会（のちに解散、一般社団法人日本能率協会に事業移管）は、「科学技術文書を英語で読む能力、書く能力、話す能力、聞く能力を客観的に正しく評価する」ための資格検定試験として、1981 年より「工業英語能力検定」を実施し、これまでに、工業高校・高等専門学校・大学等の生徒・学生や研究者、企業等において科学技術文書の作成や翻訳に携わる方々、翻訳専門会社の翻訳者など、数多くの方に受検をいただいてきました。

　一方で、当初は、我が国の主要産業である「工業」を名称に掲げましたが、工業英語能力検定の核となるテクニカル・コミュニケーションが提唱する 3C、およびパラグラフ・ライティングの考え方の有効性が実証されてくるにつれ、本国である米国では工業系にとどまらず、大半の企業、大学でテクニカル・コミュニケーションの手法を使った文書作成を推奨するようになりました。

　このような状況を鑑み、本検定の一層の普及に向けて、令和 2 年度（2020 年度）より本検定の名称を「工業英検／工業英語能力検定」から、テクニカル・コミュニケーションのより正確な訳となる「技術英検／技術英語能力検定」へと変更いたしました。本検定の目的や資格体系は現状を維持しつつ、よりわかりやすい名称へと変更することによって、理工系分野の方々のみならず幅広く訴求し、我が国のテクニカル・コミュニケーション力向上に寄与いたしたいと考えます。

〈技術英語の要となる "3C" の考え方〉

Clear（明確に）

✓ 1 回読めば理解できる英文
✓ 伝えるべき内容の論理関係を明確にした英文
✓ 具体的で分かりやすい語句と構文を使った英文

Concise（簡潔に）

✓ できるだけ少ない語数で伝わる英文
✓ 簡潔でより直接的に表現した英文
✓ 読み手の負担を最大限減らした英文

Correct（正確に）

✓ 的確な名詞や動詞が使われている英文
✓ 文法ミスや数字の間違いのない英文

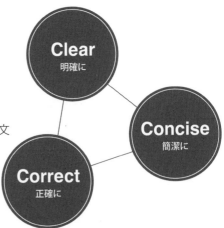

〈試験概要〉

受験資格

受験資格は一切ありません。どなたでも受験できます。

試験日

年3回実施（プロフェッショナルは年2回のみ実施）
＊詳細は下記ホームページをご確認ください。

試験形式

各級	出題形式	対象	団体受験
プロフェッショナル	記述式	科学・技術分野の英語文書を読みこなし、かつ正しく、明確に、簡潔に書くことができる。文書のスタイルは種類（マニュアル、仕様書、論文等）に応じて異なることを理解しており、正しく使いわけることができる。	×
準プロフェッショナル			
1級	選択式／記述式	科学・技術に関する英文を読むことができる。英文資料の要約、議事録、英文 E-mail 等の短文が書ける。	○
2級	選択式	科学・技術英語の語彙力があり、構文・文法を理解している。	○
3級	選択式	科学・技術英語の基礎的な語彙力があり、構文の基礎を理解している。	○

検定料（公開会場料金／税込）

プロフェッショナル	準プロフェッショナル	1級	2級	3級
￥16,500		￥6,400	￥5,300	￥2,600

＊「プロフェッショナル」「準プロフェッショナル」は同一の問題となり、得点率に応じての判定となります。

〈技術英検 1 級出題内容〉 審査基準：合計で 60％ 以上の正解 ※ 2023 年現在

No.	出題形式	問題数	配点	解答形式
Ⅰ	英単語英文解説	5	20点	マークシート方式
Ⅱ	英文空所補充 1	3	30点	
Ⅲ	短文リライト	5	30点	
Ⅳ	英文空所補充 2	4	20点	
Ⅴ	英文和訳	2	30点	記述式
Ⅵ	和文英訳	3	70点	

一般社団法人日本能率協会
JSTC 技術英語委員会

〒 105-0011 東京都港区芝公園 3-1-22

● TEL：03-3434-2350 ● E-mail：info@jstc.jp ● HP：https://jstc.jma.or.jp

〈目次〉

技術英検 1 級試験問題ならびに工業英検準 2 級試験問題

技術英検 1 級解答ならびに工業英検準 2 級解答

※ 2020 年 5 月の第 123 回技術語能力検定は、新型コロナウイルス感染拡大にともなう政府の緊急事態宣言を受け、中止いたしました。

技術英検
1級試験問題

ならびに工業英検準2級試験問題

試験時間：80分

I 次の (a) から (e) の英文の (　) に入れるべき最適な語を選び、その
番号を解答欄に記入しなさい。

(a) 3D printed (a-1) can be very complex and are ideal in a wide
(a-2) of manufacturing applications.

(a-1) 1. objection 2. objects 3. objectives
(a-2) 1. equipment 2. machine 3. variety

(b) Intellectual property rights usually give the (b-1) an exclusive
right over the use of his/her creation for a certain (b-2) of time.

(b-1) 1. examiner 2. user 3. creator
(b-2) 1. second 2. hour 3. period

(c) Wind turbines (c-1) the wind—a clean, free, and widely available
renewable energy (c-2)—to generate electric power.

(c-1) 1. make 2. cut 3. harness
(c-2) 1. source 2. consume 3. fan

(d) Knowing why landslides react the (d-1) they do to extreme
rainfall can help researchers (d-2) their future occurrence.

(d-1) 1. how 2. way 3. some
(d-2) 1. expecting 2. predict 3. pretend

(e) This liquid can be very (e-1), flowing almost like syrup, or it can
be highly stiff, (e-2) flowing at all.

(e-1) 1. fluid 2. solid 3. immovable
(e-2) 1. primitively 2. incredibly 3. scarcely

Ⅱ　次の (a) から (d) のそれぞれの英文を、情報を変えずに 3C (Correct, Clear, Concise) に則って最も簡潔に書き直した英文を 1 つ選び、その番号を解答欄に記入しなさい。

(a) Be careful, pointing the open end of a test tube containing a substance at yourself or others is dangerous.

　　1. The open end of a test tube containing a substance should be carefully pointed at yourself or others.

　　2. Be careful when pointing the open end of a test tube containing a substance at yourself or others.

　　3. Never point the open end of a test tube containing a substance at yourself or others.

(b) While digital technologies contribute to growth and drive innovation across the economy, they also bring about new risks and challenges.

　　1. Digital technologies help drive economic growth and innovation but create risks and challenges.

　　2. The digital technologies that contributed to economic growth and innovation brought new risks and challenges.

　　3. Digital technology brings new challenges, which in turn contribute to economic growth.

(c) When we talk about animal welfare, we mean the conditions in which we bring an animal to maturity.

　　1. Animal welfare is about to bring an animal to maturity.

　　2. Animal welfare refers to the conditions where an animal is raised.

　　3. Animal welfare seeks for the conditions where an animal is raised.

(d) A catalyst is a substance that can increase the rate of a chemical reaction without going through any change itself.

1. A catalyst in a chemical reaction can accelerate the rate of change in a substance.
2. A catalyst goes through a chemical reaction without delay.
3. A catalyst can hasten a chemical reaction without itself undergoing any change.

Ⅲ　次の (a) から (f) の各組の英文が同じ意味になるように、(　) に入れるべき最適な語を下の 1 から 12 より選び、その番号を解答欄に記入しなさい。なお、1 から 12 は 1 回しか使えません。

(a) We need to use a material that we can see through for this part, but we cannot find one.

A (　　　) material is needed for this part, but we cannot find one.

(b) From afar, the planet looks like a smooth marble, but in fact, its surface is very rugged.

From afar, the planet (　　　) a smooth marble, but its surface is very rugged.

(c) All the technical employees of this company need to thoroughly understand how to use the new computer system.

All the technical employees of this company need to (　　　) the information about the new computer system.

(d) ⎰ The object's axis that extends from side to side needs to be longer for a more stable spin.

⎱ The object needs a longer (　　　) axis for a more stable spin.

(e) ⎰ Experts are warning that if hurricanes continue, they might worsen the already overwhelmed drainage system.

⎱ Experts are warning that a continuation of hurricanes might (　　　) problems with the drainage system.

(f) ⎰ This house has another power system that supplies power to the house in case of a blackout.

⎱ An (　　　) power system is installed in this house in case of a blackout.

1. congregate　2. resent　　3. transit　　4. liable

5. pretends　6. transparent　7. other　　8. assimilate

9. aggravate　10. lateral　　11. resembles　12. auxiliary

Ⅳ　次の英文を読んで、各設問に答えなさい。

AAA (American Automobile Association) selected four common SUVs to evaluate the camera performance of the automatic emergency braking and lane-keeping assistance systems in simulated moderate-to-heavy rainfall.

The cars, like most new cars today, used a combination of radar sensors in the bumpers and optical cameras mounted behind the windshield. Since rain does not really affect radar, the water only needed to be sprayed over the windshields to test the cameras. It is worth noting too that the track was dry, so the tires had their ideal grip.

Researchers tested the automatic emergency braking systems of vehicles at two low, neighborhood-appropriate speeds and found that at 25 mph, 17 percent of the test runs ended in collisions. When they increased the speed to 35 mph, 33 percent of the test runs ended in collisions. The radar sensors still did their job as well as they could on their own, but without the "eyes" of the camera, it was not ideal.

The lane-keeping assist feature (**e**) far more. Test vehicles veered outside their lanes 69 percent of the time. As we know, radar cannot see lane markers, and a camera trying to **(d) peer** through heavy rain cannot really see them either.

Testers also simulated dirty windshields by stamping the glass with a concentrated solution of bugs and dirt. Interestingly, there were no negative impacts for the cameras with this smattering of sludge on the glass.

AAA has done previous research showing that these systems are not perfect. Curved lanes and high traffic can affect a car's ability to track a marked lane, and these systems cannot always see pedestrians walking at night.

All this research means that your car's radar and the camera can assist you, but they cannot yet replace you. Human brains are still the best onboard computers.

(a) 本文の内容を最もよく表しているタイトルを以下の選択肢より 1 つ選び、その番号を解答欄に記入しなさい。

1. Automatic Emergency Braking Systems Errs in Heavy Rain
2. Tests Show Driving Assistance Systems Are Not Perfect
3. Lane-Keeping Assists Cannot Replace the Driver

(b)「緊急自動ブレーキシステム」について本文の内容と合っているものを以下の選択肢より 1 つ選び、その番号を解答欄に記入しなさい。

1. カメラだけでは本当の「眼」にはならないことが分かった。
2. 大雨のときはセンサーとカメラだけでは衝突する確率が上がる。
3. カメラがないと、車の速度が上がるにつれ、衝突する確率も上がった。

(c) 本文で行われた調査の内容と合っているものを以下の選択肢より 1 つ選び、その番号を解答欄に記入しなさい。

1. カメラとレーダーの両方がないと、車線保持機能は低下する。
2. 虫や土埃がフロントガラスを覆っていると、カメラの性能が大きく下がった。
3. カーブが多い道や交通量が多い道では車線保持機能が低下する。

(d) 下線部 **(d) peer** に意味が最も近いものを以下の選択肢より 1 つ選び、その番号を解答欄に記入しなさい。

1. to read signs and analyze them
2. to find a correct way
3. to look very carefully at something

(e) (e) に入る単語を以下の選択肢より1つ選び、その番号を解答欄に記入しなさい。

1. tried
2. struggled
3. fared

V 次の英文 (a)、(b)、および (c) はそれぞれ2文で構成されています。3C (Correct, Clear, Concise) に則って内容を変えずにそれぞれ簡潔な1文でリライトしなさい。

(a) Influenza vaccines are vaccines which are often called flu shots. Influenza vaccines are vaccines that protect against the four influenza viruses.

(b) These activities are entirely beneficial. However, they do not halt the irreversible impact of carbon emissions already present in the atmosphere.

(c) Many different types of applications using this technology are under development. Examples of these applications are the measurement of air pollution, hydration levels, and blood alcohol content.

Ⅵ　次の (a) から (c) より2問選び、3C (Correct, Clear, Concise) に則って英訳しなさい。なお、選んだ2問の記号を解答欄の□に記入しなさい。□に記入がない場合は減点の対象になります。

(a) プラスチックごみは、風や雨によって川を通って海に流れ込み、波で砕かれ、紫外線で分解されて、小さなプラスチック片となる。マイクロプラスチックは、5ミリ以下の非常に小さいプラスチックごみのことを指し、近年はこのマイクロプラスチックによる海洋の生態系への影響が懸念されている。

(b) 背中のけがは、スポーツや、家の周りや庭での作業によって、または交通事故などの突然の衝撃によって負ってしまうことがある。治療の仕方はさまざまで、薬による方法、冷やす方法、ベッドで安静にする方法、そして手術などがある。健康的な体重を維持し、座っている時に腰のサポートを使用することで、背中のけがを防ぐことが出来ることもある。

(c) 当社からお届けしました製品に欠陥がありましたことをお詫びいたします。発送前にはすべての製品を検査しておりますが、それでも欠陥品が混入していることがあります。直接お持ち込みいただければ新品のものと交換させていただきます。追加の費用は一切かかりません。

第 132 回（2023.6）

I 次の (a) から (e) の英文の（　）に入れるべき最適な語を選び、その番号を解答欄に記入しなさい。

(a) Tomography is a method of (a-1) a three-dimensional image of the internal structures of a solid object (such as the human body or the (a-2)).

    (a-1)　1. consuming　　2. producing　　3. inventing
    (a-2)　1. gas　　　　　2. water　　　　3. earth

(b) (b-1) classical Euclidean geometry, a point is a primitive notion that models an exact location in the space, and has no length, width or (b-2).

    (b-1)　1. In　　　　　2. Doing　　　　3. Underneath
    (b-2)　1. weight　　　2. thickness　　3. coordinate

(c) A rainbow forms when a light wave (c-1) into multiple colors (c-2) passing through a water droplet.

    (c-1)　1. blends　　　2. diverts　　　3. splits
    (c-2)　1. before　　　2. after　　　　3. that

(d) Biometrics refers to an (d-1) system for personal identification based on one or more intrinsic (d-2) characteristics, such as fingerprints or voice patterns.

    (d-1)　1. authentication 2. audit　　　　3. evaporation
    (d-2)　1. physical　　　2. insecticide　　3. concave

(e) Soldering differs from welding in that the (e-1) is always below the melting point of the (e-2).

(e-1)　1.　humidity　　2.　temperature　3.　rigidity
(e-2)　1.　solder　　　2.　adhesive　　3.　workpiece

Ⅱ　次の (a) から (d) のそれぞれの英文を、情報を変えずに 3 C（Correct, Clear, Concise）に則って最も簡潔に書き直した英文を 1 つ選び、その番号を解答欄に記入しなさい

(a) Unlike swamps, which are dominantly covered with trees, marshes are typically treeless and covered for the most part by herbaceous plants.

1. Swamps are treeless and covered with herbaceous plants, but marshes are covered with trees.
2. Swamps are dominated by trees, whereas marshes are typically treeless and dominated by herbaceous plants.
3. Herbaceous plants dominate marshes, and shrubs dominate swamps.

(b) What filters solar radiation when violent volcanic eruptions occur is sulfur dioxide expelled into the upper layers of the earth's atmosphere by the eruptions.

1. Violent volcanic eruptions can erupt sulfur dioxide into the upper layers of the earth's atmosphere, which filters solar radiation.
2. Sulfur dioxide erupted from violent volcanos reaches the upper layers of the earth's atmosphere and release solar radiation.
3. Violent volcanic eruptions cause sulfur dioxide to be released into the earth's atmosphere.

(c) In the liquid crystal display, two pieces of polarizing filters are provided, and a liquid crystal material is provided between the polarizing filters.

  1. Two pieces of polarizing filters sandwich the liquid crystal display with a liquid crystal material.
  2. The liquid crystal display involves two pieces of polarizing filters covered with a liquid crystal material.
  3. The liquid crystal display has a liquid crystal material between two polarizing filters.

(d) If you press the Tire Pressure Monitoring button for three seconds, you will hear an audible tone.

  1. You use the Tire Pressure Monitoring button to make an audible tone for three seconds.
  2. Press the Tire Pressure Monitoring button for three seconds, and you will hear a tone.
  3. The Tire Pressure Monitoring button is used for monitoring tire pressure for a vehicle.

Ⅲ　次の (a) から (f) の各組の英文が同じ意味になるように、（　）に入れるべき最適な語を下の 1 から 12 より選び、その番号を解答欄に記入しなさい。なお、1 から 12 は 1 回しか使えません。

(a)　Building new factories in this country can be risky because the country's economy might change suddenly.

Building new factories in this country poses a risk because of its economic (　　　).

(b) ┌ The equipment's intense vibration is caused by the pistons that
　　│ move forward and backward alternately.
　　┤
　　│ The equipment's intense vibration is caused by the (　　　　)
　　└ pistons.

(c) ┌ As soon as the patient took the medicine, it made her headache
　　│ less severe.
　　┤
　　│ No sooner had the patient taken the medicine than it (　　　　)
　　└ her headache.

(d) ┌ Two roads each intersecting each other at a right angle cross
　　│ through the middle of a ranch.
　　┤
　　└ Two (　　　　) roads transverse the middle of a ranch.

(e) ┌ Ultraviolet light fulfills the function of a mutagen that is an
　　│ agent that brings about mutations in DNA.
　　┤
　　│ Ultraviolet light (　　　　) as a mutagen, an agent that
　　└ causes mutations in DNA.

(f) ┌ Preventive maintenance plays an important role in minimizing
　　│ the time during which machines are not operating.
　　┤
　　│ Preventive maintenance plays an important role in minimizing
　　└ machinery (　　　　).

1. value　　　　2. discerned　3. acts　　　　4. perpendicular
5. downtime　　6. volatility　7. switches　　8. internal
9. alleviated　10. meantime　11. reciprocating　12. repealing

19

Ⅳ　次の英文を読んで、各設問に答えなさい。

The Walkman wasn't a giant leap forward in engineering: magnetic cassette technology had been around since 1963. Sony, who (①) that point had become experts in bringing well-designed, miniaturized electronics to market (they debuted their first transistor radio in 1955), made a series of moderately successful portable cassette recorders. But the introduction of pre-recorded music tapes in the late 1960s opened a whole new market.

On July 1, 1979, Sony Corp. introduced the Sony Walkman TPS-L2, a 14 ounce, blue-and-silver, portable cassette player with chunky buttons, headphones and a leather case. It even had 【3】 second earphone jack so that two people could listen in at once. ｜a｜ Masaru Ibuka, 【4】 Sony's co-founder, traveled often for business and would find himself lugging Sony's bulky TC-D5 cassette recorder around to listen to music. He asked Norio Ohga, then Executive Deputy President, to design 【5】 playback-only stereo version, optimized for use with headphones. Ibuka brought the result — a compact, high-quality music player — to Chairman Akio Morita and reportedly said, "Try this. Don't you think a stereo cassette player that you can listen to while walking around is a good idea?"

｜b｜ Originally the Walkman was introduced in the U.S. as the "Sound-About" and in the UK as the "Stowaway," but coming up with new, uncopyrighted names in every country (②) costly; Sony eventually decided on "Walkman" as a play on the Sony Pressman, a mono cassette recorder the first Walkman prototype was based on. ｜c｜ First released in Japan, it was a massive hit: while Sony predicted it would only sell about 5,000 units a month, the Walkman sold upwards of 50,000 in the first two months. By 1986 the word "Walkman" had entered the Oxford English Dictionary. Its launch coincided with the birth of the aerobics craze, and millions used the Walkman to make their workouts more entertaining. Between 1987 and 1997 the number of people who said they walked for exercise increased by 30%.

(a) 本文の内容と合致しているものを以下の選択肢より 1 つ選び、その番号を解答欄に記入しなさい。

1. Walkman は、発売されてから最初のひと月で、50,000 台以上売れた。
2. Walkman は、70 年代、多くのユーザの提案を取り入れて作られた。
3. Walkman の前には、Pressman という商品があった。

(b) 本文から All the device needed now was a name. という一文が抜けています。この文章をいれるのに最も適切と思われる箇所を 1 つ選び解答欄に記入しなさい。

1. a
2. b
3. c

(c) （ ① ）に入る単語を 1 つ選び、その番号を解答欄に記入しなさい。

1. on
2. already
3. by

(d) （ ② ）に入る単語を 1 つ選び、その番号を解答欄に記入しなさい。

1. proved
2. ranked
3. indeed

(e) 【3】【4】【5】に入る冠詞を以下の選択肢より 1 つ選び、その番号を解答欄に記入しなさい。

1. 【3】a、【4】the、【5】a

2. 【3】the、【4】無冠詞、【5】the

3. 【3】a、【4】無冠詞、【5】a

V　次の英文メールにおいて、それぞれ 2 文で構成されている下線 (a)、(b)、および (c) を、3C (Correct, Clear, Concise) に則って内容を変えずにそれぞれ簡潔な 1 文で英訳しなさい。

工場見学の日程設定のお願い
広島工場 工場長
Lee Leo 様

(a) 4 月に予定されている、新入社員の広島工場見学の日程設定の件で連絡いたします。4 月中旬でご都合の良い日をいくつかお知らせいただければ幸いです。

(b) 今年は 30 名以上の新入社員が入社する予定です。効果的に見学できるように、2 グループに分けて実施するのがよいかもしれません。

(c) 本件に関して今月末までにご返信いただけませんでしょうか。来月上旬に参加者に日程の連絡をしたいと思っております。

よろしくお願いいたします。

日能 花子

VI　次の (a) から (c) より 2 問選び、3C (Correct, Clear, Concise) に則っ
　　て英訳しなさい。なお、選んだ 2 問の記号を解答欄の□に記入しなさい。
　　□に記入がない場合は減点の対象になります。

(a) 電波は電界と磁界が振動しながら空間を伝播するので、音や光に
　　似ている。ただ、音は空気など振動媒体がないと伝わらないが、
　　電波は宇宙空間のような真空の空間でも伝わる。伝播速度は光と
　　同じで、通り道に物質がある場合は、通り抜けたり、反射したり、
　　回折したりする。

(b) お使いの ABC 社製品に関するご質問は、製造番号と、購入店舗、
　　購入時期をご確認の上、ヘルプデスクまでお電話ください。ほと
　　んどのご質問は、訓練を積んだ当社ヘルプラインスタッフが電話
　　で解決いたします。オンラインヘルプ、サポートビデオ、一般的
　　なヒント、当社に関する情報については、当社ホームページをご
　　覧ください。

(c) 世界人口の増加により、食肉の需要は急速に拡大している。この
　　まま需要の増加が続けば、供給が追いつかなくなる可能性もある。
　　そんな中、世界的に注目されているのが『培養肉』* だ。実験室
　　で培養された動物の細胞から作られたもので、従来の食肉に代わ
　　る持続可能な食材として期待されている。
　　　［注］培養肉 * : cultured meat

第 131 回 （2023.1）

I 次の (a) から (e) の語に、それぞれ相当する記述を選び、その番号を
解答欄に記入しなさい。

(a) glacier
　1. an extremely large, floating mass of ice in the sea
　2. a large mass of ice that moves down a valley slowly
　3. a pointed piece of ice formed when water freezes as it drips

(b) vein
　1. a type of blood cell that helps the body fight infection
　2. a type of blood cell that carries oxygen to all parts of the body
　3. a tube that carries blood from all parts of the body towards the
　　heart

(c) plasticity
　1. the quality that some liquids have of being thick and sticky
　2. the ability of something to stretch and go back to its usual length
　3. the quality of being made into any shape, and of staying in that shape

(d) vaccinate
　1. to protect a person or animal from a disease by giving an
　　injection
　2. to protect people from fear of violence
　3. to supply animals with energy and nutrients

(e) synchronize
　1. to express again in the same words or terms
　2. to occur at exactly the same time
　3. to hasten the progress or development

24

Ⅱ　次の (a)、(b)、(c) の英文の（　）に入れる最適な語を下の 1 から 12 より選び、その番号を解答欄に記入しなさい。なお、1 から 12 は 1 回しか使えない。文頭に来るべき語であっても先頭は小文字になっている。

(a) (a-1) Jupiter is the largest planet in our solar system, the mass of Jupiter is only about one-thousandth (a-2) of the sun.

(b) Blood vessels are elastic tubes (b-1) which blood circulates in the body to (b-2) individual cells with oxygen and nutrients.

(c) Electromagnetic waves differ from mechanical waves (c-1) that they can travel through a vacuum and do not require a (c-2).

1. around	2. so	3. although	4. that
5. distribute	6. provide	7. in	8. spectrum
9. since	10. through	11. those	12. medium

Ⅲ　次の (a) から (e) のそれぞれの英文を、情報を変えずに最も簡潔に書き直した英文を 1 つ選び、その番号を解答欄に記入しなさい。

(a) Adoption of assisting systems in cars to support the elderly as their cognitive ability declines may soon become mandatory.

　　1. All cars may soon have to have systems that compensate for the elderly's declining cognitive abilities.
　　2. Adoption of assisting systems in vehicles that compensate for the degradation of the elderly's sensory abilities will be required.
　　3. It is mandatory to use assisting systems in cars to support the elderly with a decline in their feelings.

(b) In this chapter, the goals of this project, as well as the working mechanisms of the seismic measurement system, are clearly described.

    1. This chapter clearly projects the goals and working mechanisms of the seismic measurement system.

    2. In this chapter, the goals and mechanisms of the seismic measurement system are represented well.

    3. This chapter defines the goals of this project and describes how the seismic measurement system works.

(c) When you combine baking soda with an acid, carbon dioxide gas is produced from the baking soda.

    1. To combine with acid, baking soda produces carbon dioxide gas.

    2. When combined with an acid, the baking soda carbonates dioxide gas.

    3. Combining baking soda with an acid produces carbon dioxide gas.

(d) The sum of the squares of the lengths of the two short sides of a right-angled triangle is equal to the square of the length of the longest side.

    1. In a regular triangle, the square of the hypotenuse is the sum of the squares of the other two sides.

    2. In a right-angled triangle, the length of the longest side squared is the sum of the squares of the other two sides.

    3. The square of the longest side of a right-angled triangle is the square root of the other two sides.

(e) During replication, the two strands of DNA are separated into unpaired strands, and each strand acts as a template for the synthesis of the other strand.

    1. During DNA replication, DNA produces exact templates of itself through synthesis.

    2. During replication, the two strands of DNA are unwound, each becoming a template for the other.

    3. During replication, the two strands of DNA produce two kinds of templates for the synthesis of DNA.

Ⅳ　次の (a) から (d) の各組の英文が同じ意味になるように、（　）に入れ
　　る最適な語を下の 1 から 12 より選び、その番号を解答欄に記入しなさ
　　い。なお、1 から 12 は 1 回しか使えない。文頭に来るべき語であって
　　も先頭は小文字になっている。

(a)　The engine developed recently is designed to save fuel use by
　　　10%, compared with the previous model.

　　　The newly developed engine is designed to have a (　　　　　)
　　　10% better than the old one.

(b)　The collapse of the building was caused by the weakness of
　　　the steel structure.

　　　The weakness of the steel structure (　　　) to the collapse of
　　　the building.

(c)　The amount of energy delivered to the earth's surface by
　　　overhead sunlight is in the vicinity of 1 kW per square meter.

　　　Overhead sunlight delivers (　　　) 1 kW per square meter
　　　to the earth's surface.

(d)　The freezing point of water is 0°C and the boiling point of
　　　water is 100°C.

　　　(　　　) water freezes at 0°C, it boils at 100°C.

1.　during	2.　led	3.　gasoline	4.　lead
5.　while	6.　due	7.　meanwhile	8.　approximately
9.　biomass	10. exactly	11. mileage	12. relatively

V 次の (a)、(b) より 1 問選び、和訳しなさい。なお、選んだ 1 問の記号を解答欄の□に記入しなさい。□の記入がない場合は減点の対象になります。

(a) The three elements of sound are pitch, loudness, and tone. Pitch is determined by the frequency of the sound waves. The higher the frequency is, the higher the pitch becomes; the lower the frequency, the lower the pitch. Humans can hear sound with frequencies between 20 Hz and 20,000 Hz. Sound lower than 20 Hz is called infrasound,* whereas sound higher than 20,000 Hz is called ultrasound. Animals like bats can use ultrasound to detect objects and navigate their way through the darkness.

［注］infrasound *：超低周波音

(b) The 2D and 3D printing processes are basically the same: multiple layers are laid down on the same place to form something —sakinia 2D printer draws a picture and a 3D printer builds a solid model. A 3D CAD drawing is turned into many two-dimensional cross-sectional layers, and a 3D printer prints one layer at a time over and over again, working from the bottom and making its way upward. It can take hours to build up a model.

Ⅵ　次の (a) から (c) より 2 問選び、英訳しなさい。なお、選んだ 2 問の
　　記号を解答欄の□に記入しなさい。□の記入がない場合は減点の対象
　　になります。

(a) 人工的知覚技術の発達は目覚ましい。今では、光学センサーで個
　　人を識別したり、自律走行車が適切な速度で公道を走ったり、ロ
　　ボットがビルの中を歩き回って空き缶を集めたりすることができ
　　るようになっている。

(b) 世界の石油需要と温室効果ガス排出量は、2019 年にピークを迎え
　　た可能性がある。なぜなら、感染症の流行が経済成長を減速させ、
　　脱炭素を加速させ、またテレワークを継続せざるを得なくなり、
　　エネルギー需要が長期的に減少する可能性があるからである。

(c) 温度は物質にさまざまな影響を与える。物質が高温になると、分
　　子が速く動くようになり、特性が変化する。物質の物理的な状態は、
　　温度によって影響を受ける。例えば、水は 0℃ 以下では固体、0℃
　　を超えると液体、100℃ では気体に変化する。

I　次の (a) から (e) の語に、それぞれ相当する記述を選び、その番号を
解答欄に記入しなさい。

(a) degenerative
1. capable of producing substances chemically or biologically
2. marked by gradual deterioration of organs and cells
3. the breakdown of food into smaller components that can be absorbed

(b) inhibitor
1. a substance that retards or stops a chemical reaction
2. a substance or agent used to kill insects and other arthropods
3. a substance that produces hydrogen ions

(c) tangible
1. unreal and existing only in imagination or mind
2. completely flat and even, free from rough areas
3. clear enough or definite enough to be easily seen, felt, or noticed

(d) precipitate
1. a solid material separated from a solution especially by a chemical process
2. any of the large systems of stars in outer space
3. an organic compound consisting of hydrogen and carbon

(e) eclipse
1. an object that is completely round in shape
2. a partial or whole obscuring of one celestial body by another
3. an oval shape similar to a circle but longer and flatter

Ⅱ　次の (a)、(b)、(c) の英文の （　） に入れる最も適切な語を下の 1 か
　　ら 12 より選び、その番号を解答欄に記入しなさい。なお、1 から 12
　　は 1 回しか使えない。

(a) Although (　a-1　) and viruses are both too small to be seen
without a microscope, they're as (　a-2　) as giraffes are from
goldfish.

(b) It is important to distinguish (　b-1　) minor earthquakes that cause
no damage and major earthquakes that (　b-2　) in horrific loss of
life.

(c) The manufacturer of the air purifier recommends that the filter
(　c-1　) cleaned twice a month to ensure (　c-2　) performance.

1.　optimal	2.　result	3.　hit	4.　the same
5.　bacteria	6.　are	7.　be	8.　different
9.　mites	10. between	11. from	12. low

Ⅲ　次の (a) から (e) のそれぞれの英文を情報を変えずに最も簡潔に書き
　　直した英文を 1 つ選び、その番号を解答欄に記入しなさい。

(a) A pandemic of influenza occurs at a time when a new influenza
virus to which no human population has the immunity appears.

1. A flu pandemic occurs when a new flu virus appears and
humans have no immunity to it.
2. A flu pandemic occurs when a new flu virus to which humans
are immune appears.
3. An influenza pandemic occurs when humans appear to have no
immunity to a new virus.

(b) In order to ensure the reliability of high current power devices, for automotive applications in particular, it is critical to ensure the quality of SiC wafers.

　1. The quality of SiC wafers is critical to ensure the dependability of high-current power devices in automotive applications.

　2. The quality of SiC wafers is critical for the reliability of high-current power devices, particularly those used in automobiles.

　3. High quality SiC wafers are critical for increased performance of high-current power devices used in particular automobiles.

(c) If the rider uses pedal-assist mode, the rider is helped by the power from the motor and the pedaling is made easy.

　1. Using pedal-assist mode, the rider can powerfully pedal the motor.

　2. Pedal-assist mode helps the rider use less power from the motor.

　3. In pedal-assist mode, the motor provides power and makes pedaling easier.

(d) Heme-iron can be taken in by the human body in a more efficient way than non-heme iron can.

　1. Non-heme iron is absorbed by the human body more effectively than heme-iron.

　2. The human body can absorb heme-iron more efficiently than non-heme iron.

　3. The human body can adsorb to heme-iron more efficiently than non-heme iron.

(e) The area of a circle can be calculated by the radius times the radius times pi.

　1. To obtain the area of a circle, the circumference is multiplied by pi.

　2. The area of a circle equals to a multiplication of the radius and pi.

　3. The area of a circle is pi times the radius squared.

Ⅳ　次の (a) から (d) の各組の英文が同じ意味になるように、（　）に入れる最も適切な語を下の 1 から 12 より選び、その番号を解答欄に記入しなさい。なお、1 から 12 は 1 回しか使えない。

(a)　Many smart devices are designed to be small enough to be carried by one person.

　　Many smart devices are (　　　　) small that one person can carry them.

(b)　A mixture is a substance in which two or more substances are physically mixed without chemical reactions.

　　A mixture (　　　　) two or more substances that are not chemically combined.

(c)　Many mechanical devices such as oil jacks and hydraulic brakes work according to this theory.

　　This theory (　　　　) to many mechanical devices such as oil jacks and hydraulic brake systems.

(d)　In the AI development process, the programming of human-like characteristics is often carried out.

　　The AI development process often (　　　　) the programming of human-like characteristics.

1.　controls　　2.　relatively　　3.　attains　　4.　applies

5.　so　　6.　conforms　　7.　too　　8.　refers

9.　involves　　10. delivers　　11. complicates　　12. contains

V 次の (a)、(b) より 1 問選び、和訳しなさい。なお、選んだ 1 問の記号を解答欄の□に記入しなさい。□の記入がない場合は減点の対象になります。

(a) A ray of light passing into a transparent material such as a glass plate only goes straight through if it strikes the material at right angles. Otherwise, the direction of the ray changes, because the material refracts it. The change in angle is different depending on the material. What indicates this difference is the refractive index* of the material. The bigger the refractive index, the greater the change of direction. When the light ray enters the material, it slows down. The speed of light in the material is reduced in proportion to the refractive index.

［注］refractive index* : 屈折率

(b) The core function of a Global Positioning System (GPS)* receiver is to enable its users to locate their precise geographical position. To allow precise positioning, the device is designed to receive separate signals from three or more satellites at altitudes of approximately 20,000 km. These signals contain information about the orbits of the satellites and the time of atomic clocks onboard. By comparing the arrival times, or the time delays between transmission and reception, the GPS receiver computes its current location.

［注］Global Positioning System (GPS)* : 全地球測位システム（GPS）

Ⅵ　次の (a) から (c) より 2 問選び、英訳しなさい。なお、選んだ 2 問の
　　記号を解答欄の□に記入しなさい。□の記入がない場合は減点の対象
　　になります。

(a) すべての生物は細胞で構成されている。すべての細胞には核があ
　　り、核の中に染色体 * が含まれ、ヒトの場合、一つの核あたりに
　　２３対の染色体がある。子が親に似るのは、染色体にある遺伝子
　　によって親から子に生物学的情報が伝わるからである。
　　[注] 染色体 * : chromosome

(b) バイオマス発電では、植物残さ * 等のバイオマスを燃料として発
　　電を行う。バイオマスを燃焼した場合でも CO_2 は発生するが、植
　　物はその CO_2 を吸収して成長し、バイオマスに戻すので、大気中
　　の CO_2 の量は増加しないと考えられる。つまり、カーボンニュー
　　トラルであると見なすことができる。
　　[注] 残さ * : residue

(c) 無線 LAN には 2.4GHz 帯、5GHz 帯および 60GHz 帯の周波数が割
　　り当てられている。ほとんどの無線 LAN 機器は Wi-Fi 認証を得て
　　おり、Wi-Fi ロゴを与えられている。Wi-Fi ロゴを持つ製品であれば、
　　家電製品でも、スマートフォンでも無線 LAN に接続することがで
　　きる。

第 129 回（2022.6）

I　次の (a) から (e) の語に、それぞれ相当する記述を選び、その番号を
解答欄に記入しなさい。

(a) malignant
1. motivated by wrongful, vicious, or mischievous purposes
2. grand or noble in thought or accomplishment
3. arranged in a straight line or in correct positions

(b) habitat
1. the environment in which an animal or plant normally lives
2. an activity pursued in spare time for pleasure or relaxation
3. a recurrent pattern of behavior acquired through frequent
repetition

(c) tilt
1. to rise to a higher position or level
2. to move into a position with one side higher than the other
3. to put or place things one on top of another

(d) pierce
1. to force or shape something straight into a curve
2. to drive, push or force something back or away
3. to make a small hole in something, using a sharp object

(e) median
1. the middle value of a set of numbers arranged in order
2. the main part of a group of people or things
3. a number that can be divided only by itself and 1

Ⅱ　次の (a)、(b)、(c) の英文の（　）に入れる最適な語を下の 1 から 12 より選び、その番号を解答欄に記入しなさい。なお、1 から 12 は 1 回しか使えない。

(a) Scientists have attempted to explain how electromagnetic （ a-1) can display duality, or (a-2) particle-like and wave-like behavior.

(b) Carbon dioxide is (b-1) from the atmosphere when it is absorbed by (b-2) as part of the biological carbon cycle.

(c) Deep (c-1) attempts to mimic the human (c-2), enabling systems to cluster data and make predictions with incredible accuracy.

1. learning	2. either	3. resources	4. plants
5. removed	6. seawater	7. radiation	8. generated
9. fake	10. both	11. brain	12. absorption

Ⅲ　次の (a) から (e) のそれぞれの英文を情報を変えずに最も簡潔に書き直した英文を 1 つ選び、その番号を解答欄に記入しなさい。

(a) When a voltage is applied to a diode, the electrons in the diode are caused to start to move in a single direction.

　　1. A voltage applied to a diode causes electronic singularity to start in the diode.
　　2. A voltage applied to a diode makes the diode start to move its electrons singularly.
　　3. A voltage applied to a diode makes the electrons in it move in one direction.

(b) In conducting research and development in materials science, it is an important element to make an effective use of four-dimensional big data.

   1. Materials science requires four-dimensional data for its research and development.

   2. Effective use of four-dimensional big data is important for research and development in materials science.

   3. Effective four-dimensional big data is used for research and development in materials science.

(c) When a lightning strike occurs and heats the surrounding air rapidly, the rapidly heated air produces a sound called thunder.

   1. Thunder is the lightning strike that occurs and heats the surrounding air rapidly.

   2. What produces thunder is a lightning strike that makes a sound.

   3. Thunder is the sound produced by the air rapidly heated around a lightning strike.

(d) When fossil fuels are burned, air pollution is generated as this process produces such substances as sulfur dioxide and carbon dioxide.

   1. Burning fossil fuels produces sulfur dioxide and carbon dioxide, leading to air pollution.

   2. Fossil fuels cause air pollution as sulfur dioxide and carbon dioxide are burned.

   3. Sulfur dioxide and carbon dioxide pollute from heated fossil fuels.

(e) According to a law called Young's Modulus of Elasticity, a percentage increase in stress will cause the same percentage increase in strain.

   1. According to Young's Modulus of Elasticity, stress is equal to strain.

   2. According to Young's Modulus of Elasticity, stress is proportional to strain.

   3. According to Young's Modulus of Elasticity, stress and strain are constant.

Ⅳ　次の (a) から (d) の各組の英文が同じ意味になるように、(　　　) に
　　入れる最適な語を下の 1 から 12 より選び、その番号を解答欄に記入し
　　なさい。なお、1 から 12 は 1 回しか使えない。

(a)　Productivity can be improved by networks, because they allow
　　　workers to share information easily.

　　　Networks increase productivity (　　　) allowing workers to
　　　share information easily.

(b)　A primary color filter for digital cameras enhances the color
　　　reception of red, green, and blue wavelengths of light.

　　　Using a primary color filter (　　　) the color reception of
　　　red, green and blue in digital cameras.

(c)　Since children require more protein per kilogram of body weight
　　　than adults, they are prone to the influence of protein deficiency.

　　　Since children require more protein per kilogram of body weight
　　　than adults, they are more (　　　) to protein deficiency.

(d)　The earth's magnetic field is currently pointing in a direction which
　　　is different from the direction in which it pointed in times long past.

　　　The earth's magnetic field is currently pointing in a direction
　　　different from (　　　) it was in times long past.

1.　decouples　　2.　when　　　　3.　by　　　　4.　coherent

5.　indispensable　6.　amplifies　　7.　for　　　　8.　what

9.　susceptible　　10. once　　　　11. simplifies　12. one

V 次の (a)、(b) より 1 問選び、和訳しなさい。なお、選んだ 1 問の記号を解答欄の□に記入しなさい。□の記入がない場合は減点の対象になります。

(a) Fiber optic cables carry data as pulses of light. Light transmitted through them can travel over extended distances. The pulses of light are not affected by electromagnetic radiation, so fiber optic cables are thus suitable for environments with large amounts of electrical interference. The transmission speed of a fiber optic cable is thousands of times more than that of a twisted-pair wire.* This has enabled large-capacity video conferencing and other interactive services and helped broaden communication possibilities.

［注］twisted-pair wire* : より対線

(b) A meta-analysis was conducted for the six major randomized trials of aspirin for primary prevention of vascular disease.* Among more than 95,000 participants, serious cardiovascular events occurred in 0.51% of participants taking aspirin and 0.57% of those not taking aspirin. This corresponds to an 11% relative reduction in risk. At the same time, serious bleeding events increased from 0.07% among non-aspirin takers to 0.10% among those taking aspirin, or a 43% relative increase in risk.

［注］vascular disease* : 血管疾患

Ⅵ　次の（a）から（c）より 2 問選び、英訳しなさい。なお、選んだ 2 問の記号を解答欄の□に記入しなさい。□の記入がない場合は減点の対象になります。

(a) クリーンルームとは、温度と湿度が厳密に管理された、埃のない作業場のことで、電子機器や航空宇宙 * システム部品など、不純物による汚染の影響を受けやすい機器の研究や製造において、非常に重要な役割を果たす。
［注］航空宇宙 * : aerospace

(b) 炭水化物 * などの有機物が酸素と結合すると、二酸化炭素と水が生成されると共に熱が放出される。この熱エネルギーは、何もないところから生まれるのではなく、有機物がもともと持っていた他のエネルギーから変換されたものである。
［注］炭水化物 * : carbohydrates

(c) 宇宙ごみは *、軌道周回をしている不要な人工物体のことである。運用を終えた人工衛星や、故障した人工衛星、打ち上げロケットの上段部分、爆発や衝突により発生した破片などがある。現在、地上から追跡されている 10cm 以上の物体で 2 万個ほどあり、将来の宇宙活動の妨げになる恐れがある。
［注］宇宙ごみ * : space debris

第 128 回 （2022. 1）

I 次の (a) から (e) の語に、それぞれ相当する記述を選び、その番号を
解答欄に記入しなさい。

(a) latitude
  1. a structure of crossed wooden or metal strips
  2. distance east or west of the Greenwich meridian on the earth's surface
  3. distance north or south of the equator on the earth's surface

(b) cultivate
  1. to grow or maintain living cells or tissue in culture
  2. to develop over time into forms better adapted to survive
  3. to change or make something change from one form to another

(c) convection
  1. a phenomenon in which a gas becomes a liquid
  2. the circulation movement of a gas or liquid
  3. a very strong belief or opinion on a matter

(d) irradiate
  1. to expose someone or something to radioactivity
  2. to reflect heat, light, or electromagnetic waves
  3. to make someone feel annoyed or impatient by disturbance

(e) base
  1. any compounds which are capable of reacting with oxygen to form water
  2. a chemical compound that combines with an acid to form a salt and water
  3. any elements that are dissolved to form a crystal

Ⅱ　次の (a)、(b)、(c) の英文の（　）に入れる最適な語を下の 1 から 12 より選び、その番号を解答欄に記入しなさい。なお、1 から 12 は 1 回しか使えない。

(a) Photovoltaic (　a-1　) use light energy (photons) from the sun to generate (　a-2　) through the photovoltaic effect.

(b) Kelvin (K) is the (　b-1　) of temperature on the absolute scale and is named (　b-2　) William Thomson, 1st Baron Kelvin.

(c) Astronomy is the field of science (　c-1　) deals with the study of (　c-2　) bodies such as stars, comets, planets, and galaxies.

1.　to	2.　after	3.　heat	4.　celestial
5.　electricity	6.　where	7.　item	8.　unit
9.　that	10. cellars	11. cells	12. biological

Ⅲ　次の (a) から (e) のそれぞれの英文を情報を変えずに最も簡潔に書き直した英文を 1 つ選び、その番号を解答欄に記入しなさい。

(a) The soil microbes change the forms of organic nutrients so that they are easily available.

1. The soil microbes transform organic nutrients into easily available forms.
2. The soil microbes change organic nutrients that are easy to use.
3. Organic nutrients are transformed into easily available soil microbes.

(b) As one of the top ocean predators, sharks play a role in helping ensure that the balance of the ocean's ecosystem is maintained.

  1. Sharks are among the top ocean predators and help maintain the balance of the ocean's ecosystem.
  2. It is the most dangerous sharks that play the role of maintaining the balance of the ocean's ecosystem.
  3. The balance of the ocean's ecosystem is maintained by sharks, the most helping predators.

(c) Velocity is the same as speed, except for the fact that velocity also indicates the direction of motion.

  1. Velocity is the same as speed despite the direction of motion.
  2. Like speed, velocity indicates the direction of motion.
  3. Velocity is speed with the direction of motion

(d) With carbon dioxide and water, organic compounds are produced by green plants in the presence of sunlight. Such a chemical process is called photosynthesis.

  1. Photosynthesis is a chemical process by which green plants are carbonized in sunlight.
  2. Photosynthesis is a chemical process by which green plants produce carbon dioxide and water in sunlight.
  3. Photosynthesis is a chemical process by which green plants produce organic compounds from carbon dioxide and water under sunlight.

(e) In arteries, blood containing oxygen flows away from the heart. In veins, blood from which oxygen was removed flows toward the heart.

  1. Arteries and veins exchange oxygen in the blood to and from the heart.
  2. Arteries carry oxygenated blood from the heart, and veins carry deoxygenated blood to the heart.
  3. Blood with oxygen flows through veins, and blood without oxygen flows through arteries.

Ⅳ　次の (a) から (d) の各組の英文が同じ意味になるように、(　　　) に入れる最適な語を下の 1 から 12 より選び、その番号を解答欄に記入しなさい。なお、1 から 12 は 1 回しか使えない。

(a) ⎰ The sensors for detecting an approaching object must be installed at least 5 cm from each other.

⎱ The (　　　) sensors must be installed at least 5 cm apart.

(b) ⎰ Many factories in this area are not making profits anymore.

⎱ Many factories in this area are no longer economically (　　　).

(c) ⎰ All these methods have a process in which an equilibrium is disturbed by rapid changes in temperature or pressure.

⎱ All these methods (　　　) disturbing an equilibrium by rapid changes in temperature or pressure.

(d) ⎰ One of the issues with an aging society is an increase of elderly people with a mental disorder associated with the ability to think.

⎱ An issue with an aging society is an increase in elderly people with a (　　　) disorder.

1. achieve　　2. synchronous　3. depression　4. proximity
5. viable　　6. bankrupt　　7. independent　8. cognitive
9. nutritional　10. involve　　11. resolve　　12. tactile

V 次の (a)、(b) より 1 問選び、和訳しなさい。なお、選んだ 1 問の記号を解答欄の□に記入しなさい。□の記入がない場合は減点の対象になります。

(a) The atmosphere serves to moderate the extremes of heat and cold on the earth. As the heat of the sun penetrates the air and warms the earth's surface during the day, the atmosphere traps this heat. The heat escapes slowly into space, making the night warmer than it would be without this effect. The atmosphere also protects the earth's inhabitants to some extent from meteor particles,* cosmic rays, radiation from the sun and stars, and other hazards.
　［注］meteor particles*: 流星粒子

(b) Radiators are used in cooling systems, for example, in vehicle engines. Coolant is pumped around the hot engine to absorb heat and travels through a radiator provided in the vehicle. As the vehicle moves, wind hits the radiator to cool the radiator and the coolant inside it. Without a cooling system, the engine would overheat. This, however, would not happen immediately after starting the engine due to thermal inertia;* it takes time to change the temperature of a body with a large mass.
　［注］thermal inertia*: 熱慣性

Ⅵ　次の (a) から (c) より２問選び、英訳しなさい。なお、選んだ２問の
　　記号を解答欄の□に記入しなさい。□の記入がない場合は減点の対象
　　になります。

(a) 科学的発見からビジネスインテリジェンスまで、データサイエン
　　スは私たちの世界を変えつつある。情報のデジタル化、センサー
　　の普及、機械学習と可視化 * の進歩、コストや帯域幅、スケーラビ
　　リティの劇的な向上などの著しい変化が相まって、大きなチャン
　　スが生まれている。
　　［注］可視化 * : visualization

(b) ホッキョクグマは、狩猟、移動、繁殖 * など、生活のほぼすべての
　　面において海氷に依存している。NASA の衛星は海氷の変化を追
　　跡しており、そのデータによると、1979 年から 2019 年の間に北極
　　の海氷が年平均約 53,100 ㎢ のペースで縮小している。
　　［注］繁殖 * : breeding

(c) 懸濁液（サスペンション）とは、分散した小さな固体粒子を含む
　　液体のことです。例えば、容器に水と土を入れて振ると、懸濁液
　　になります。固体粒子は、懸濁液をろ過すると残渣 * として回収さ
　　れ、放置するとゆっくりと容器の底に沈み沈殿物 ** を形成します。
　　［注］残渣 * : residue　　　沈殿物 ** : sediment

第 127 回（2021. 11）

I　次の (a) から (e) の語に、それぞれ相当する記述を選び、その番号を
　　解答欄に記入しなさい。

(a) embryo
1. a plant or animal at an early stage of its development
2. an order prohibiting the departure or arrival of merchant ships
3. an act of holding close with the arms

(b) calibrate
1. to mark the scale of a measuring instrument
2. to check the accuracy of mathematical calculations
3. to maintain the balance of the earth's ecosystem

(c) emission
1. a gas thought to cause the greenhouse effect
2. a gas found under the ground or under the sea
3. a gas or other substance sent out into the air

(d) conform
1. to transform materials into unusual shapes
2. to give information to an authority
3. to obey a law, rule, or specifications

(e) immunology
1. the branch of biology which is concerned with very small living things
2. the branch of science dealing with antigens and antibodies
3. the scientific study of people, society, and culture

Ⅱ　次の (a)、(b)、(c) の英文の (　) に入れる最も適切な語を下の 1 か
　　ら 12 より選び、その番号を解答欄に記入しなさい。なお、1 から 12
　　は 1 回しか使えない。

(a) As with any triangle, the area is (　a-1　) to one half the base
　　multiplied (　a-2　) the corresponding height.

(b) Rocket engines work by action and reaction; they push rockets
　　(　b-1　) simply by expelling their exhaust in the (　b-2　) direction
　　at high speed.

(c) A coupling is a mechanical device used (　c-1　) connect two shafts
　　and transmit torque from one shaft to the (　c-2　).

1. front	2. by	3. with	4. opposite
5. forward	6. for	7. to	8. normal
9. similar	10. equal	11. other	12. another

Ⅲ　次の (a) から (e) のそれぞれの英文を情報を変えずに最も簡潔に書き
　　直した英文を 1 つ選び、その番号を解答欄に記入しなさい。

(a) The reaction of this camera to the movements of the subject is
　　very quick in any situation.

　　1. This camera can be used for quick photographic processing of
　　　the subject.
　　2. This camera can move quickly to capture the subject.
　　3. This camera is highly responsive to the movements of the
　　　subject in any situation.

(b) Scientists have discovered microplastics that are floating in the waters near a coastal coral reef that is listed as a World Heritage site.

    1. Microplastics are discovered by scientists floating at a coral reef at a World Heritage listed site.

    2. Microplastics discovered by scientists in the waters near the World Heritage coral reef were listed.

    3. Scientists have discovered microplastics in the waters near a coastal coral reef listed as a World Heritage site.

(c) If you use pulse oximetry, it is easy and painless to see how well oxygen is sent to parts of your body.

    1. Pulse oximetry is an easy, painless measure to see the oxygen level in your body.

    2. With pulse oximetry, it is easy to remove pain caused by oxygen in your body.

    3. Pulse oximetry can be used painlessly to see how the oxygen level in your body easily changes.

(d) There are sometimes changes in DNA sequences, and they are called mutations, and the mutations can cause problems such as diseases.

    1. Changes in DNA sequences are sometimes called mutations that can cause diseases.

    2. Occasional changes in DNA, called mutations, can cause problems including diseases.

    3. Changes in DNA sequences can cause problems such as mutations.

(e) When a stretching force is applied to a material, the shape of the material can be changed.

    1. Stretching can deform a material.

    2. Stretching a material forces it to change its shape.

    3. Stretching force can be applied to the change of the material.

Ⅳ　次の (a) から (d) の各組の英文が同じ意味になるように、( ) に入れ
る最も適切な語を下の 1 から 12 より選び、その番号を解答欄に記入し
なさい。なお、1 から 12 は 1 回しか使えない。

(a) ⎰ Machines need to be repaired when they are not working correctly.

⎱ Machines need ( ) when they are out of order.

(b) ⎰ You can limit your intake of small amounts of pesticide that remain
on fruits and vegetables by peeling or thoroughly washing them.

⎱ You can limit your intake of pesticide ( ) by peeling or
thoroughly washing fruits and vegetables.

(c) ⎰ Natural killer cells are a type of lymphoid cell that recognizes
and destroys tissue cells affected with virus.

⎱ Natural killer cells are a type of lymphoid cell that recognizes
and destroys virus-( ) tissue cells.

(d) ⎰ As a result of the investigation, we found the hypothesis that the filter
clogging was the cause of the performance degradation to be correct.

⎱ Our investigation ( ) that the filter clogging caused the
performance degradation.

1. confirmed　2. recognized　3. repairing　4. repaired
5. effected　6. absorption　7. pollution　8. infected
9. to repair　10. residues　11. denied　12. free

V 次の (a)、(b) より 1 問選び、和訳しなさい。なお、選んだ 1 問の記号を解答欄の□に記入しなさい。□の記入がない場合は減点の対象になります。

(a) The fauna* of Japan is close to that of the Eurasian Continent. This is due to the migration of animals from the continents during the ice age when the Japanese archipelago** was connected to the mainland. However, there is a significant difference in fauna between the Yakushima-Tanegashima Islands and Amamioshima Island, reflecting the history of repeated connections with and separations of these islands from the continent. These historically and geographically isolated islands are inhabited by many endemic species***.

［注］fauna* : 動物相　　Japanese archipelago** : 日本列島　　endemic species*** : 固有種

(b) ROM refers to computer memory chips containing permanent data. ROM is non-volatile*: the data is retained in it even after the computer is turned off. In ROM, critical programs such as the basic input/output system (BIOS) are stored, which is used to boot up the computer when it is turned on. The BIOS consists of a few kilobytes of code that instructs the computer what to do when it starts up, such as running hardware diagnostics and loading the operating system into the RAM.

［注］fnon-volatile* : 不揮発性の

Ⅵ　次の (a) から (c) より 2 問選び、英訳しなさい。なお、選んだ 2 問の記号を解答欄の□に記入しなさい。□の記入がない場合は減点の対象になります。

(a) 溶接とは、金属部品を溶けるまで加熱して押さえることで、部材同士を接合する方法である。材料によっては、高熱にさらされると性質が変化したり、劣化したりする恐れがあるため、溶接を行う際は、部材に所定の規格に定められた耐久性があることを確認する必要がある。

(b) 一般的に、鉄筋コンクリートに使用される鋼は、事前に水や、空気中の酸素にさらされている。その結果、こうした鋼は通常部分的に腐食しており、酸化鉄 * の層で覆われている。しかし、鋼はいったん硬化したコンクリートの内部に入ると、空気と水から保護されるようになり、その結果、さらなる酸化を防ぐことになる。
[注] 酸化鉄 * : iron oxide

(c) 周波数は、単位時間内にある固定点を通過する波の数、または周期的な動きのある物体の単位時間あたりの周期または振動の数です。周波数の最も一般的な単位はヘルツであり、1 Hz は、毎秒 1 周期であることを示します。

第 126 回（2021. 6）

I　次の (a) から (e) の語に、それぞれ相当する記述を選び、その番号を解答欄に記入しなさい。

(a) hydroxide
　　1. a base or alkali containing the ion OH⁻
　　2. a substance that increases the rate of a chemical reaction
　　3. any organic compound containing only carbon and hydrogen

(b) backlash
　　1. a yard located at the back of a house
　　2. an ache or pain in the back, especially the lower back
　　3. a reaction between badly fitting parts in a mechanism

(c) amputate
　　1. to cut down trees for lumber
　　2. to remove part of the body by cutting
　　3. to disconnect an electrical device

(d) irrigate
　　1. to remove or draw off water from a place
　　2. to supply water to land or crops to help growth
　　3. to sprinkle water over an industrial plant or facility

(e) centrifugal
　　1. moving or tending to move away from a center
　　2. having the same center
　　3. having an edge in the shape of a circle

Ⅱ　次の (a)、(b)、(c) の英文の（　）に入れる最適な語を下の 1 から 12 より選び、その番号を解答欄に記入しなさい。なお、1 から 12 は 1 回しか使えない。

(a) Magnesium is an important nutrient for the human body; chronic magnesium (　a-1　) can increase the risk (　a-2　) heart disease and diabetes.

(b) (　b-1　) most organisms cannot live at extremely high temperatures, certain species can (　b-2　) temperatures up to 120°C.

(c) Fuel cells generate power through an (　c-1　) process. They convert chemical energy to electrical energy by (　c-2　) hydrogen and oxygen from the air.

1. although　　　2. calibrate　　3. combining　4. since
5. electromechanical 6. deficiency 7. intake　　　8. of
9. on　　　　　　10. mixing　　　11. tolerate　　12. electrochemical

Ⅲ　次の (a) から (e) のそれぞれの英文を情報を変えずに最も簡潔に書き直した英文を 1 つ選び、その番号を解答欄に記入しなさい。

(a) When organic substances, which contain carbon molecules, are burned, carbon dioxide and water vapor are produced.

1. Carbon dioxide and water vapor are produced when burning organic substances contain carbon molecules.
2. Burning organic substances produces carbon dioxide and water vapor.
3. When organically substituted carbon molecules are burned, carbon dioxide and water vapor are produced.

(b) The speed of sound refers to the speed at which the sound moves, which is the speed at which the energy travels, between two places.

    1. Sound moves between two places, which is the speed of its energy.

    2. The speed of sound is how fast the sound, or its energy, travels between two places.

    3. Sound and its energy move between two places at high speed.

(c) By introducing new types of technology, it became possible for manufacturers to design intelligent industrial machines.

    1. Introducing the new technology allowed to design manufacturers' intelligent industrial machines.

    2. The introduction of the new technology by manufacturers permitted to design intelligent industrial machines.

    3. New technology enabled manufacturers to make industrial machines intelligent.

(d) As we get older with age, the amount of visible light that passes through the eye lenses becomes smaller.

    1. As we get older, less visible light passes through the eye lenses.

    2. Visible light that passes through the human eye lenses becomes smaller with age.

    3. The eye lenses of the elderly transmit more visible light than the young.

(e) When a beam of light hits a mirror, the mirror reflects the beam of light.

    1. A mirror reflects light when it hits the light.

    2. A beam of light hits a mirror and reflects it.

    3. A beam of light is reflected when it hits a mirror.

Ⅳ 次の (a) から (d) の各組の英文が同じ意味になるように、(　　　) に
　　入れる最適な語を下の 1 から 12 より選び、その番号を解答欄に記入し
　　なさい。なお、1 から 12 は 1 回しか使えない。文頭に来るべき語であっ
　　ても先頭は小文字になっている。

(a) ┌ Liquids and gases are made up of tiny, constantly moving
　　│ particles called molecules.
　　┤
　　│ Liquids and gases (　　　　　) of tiny, constantly moving
　　└ particles called molecules.

(b) ┌ Some butterflies have protective coloration and can make
　　│ themselves invisible to predators.
　　┤
　　│ Some butterflies manage to escape a predator's detection by
　　└ (　　　　) with the background.

(c) ┌ An X-ray inspection, generally used in production, is a test that
　　│ does not damage a product being tested.
　　┤
　　│ An X-ray inspection is a (　　　　　) test generally used in
　　└ production.

(d) ┌ In contrast with conventional vehicles that just use fossil fuels,
　　│ electric vehicles use an electric motor.
　　┤
　　│ (　　　　　) conventional vehicles that just use fossil fuels,
　　└ electric vehicles use an electric motor.

1.　unlike　　　　2.　comprise　　　　3.　inducing　4.　merging

5.　unless　　　　6.　non-combustible　7.　compose　8.　non-breakable

9.　non-destructive　10. consist　　　　11. except　　12. confusing

V 次の (a)、(b) より 1 問選び、和訳しなさい。なお、選んだ 1 問の記号を解答欄の□に記入しなさい。□の記入がない場合は減点の対象になります。

(a) Hydroforming* is a way of shaping materials such as aluminum or ultralight steel. The metal is pushed into shape using fluid pressure. For example, to produce components for car bodies, steel tubes are placed inside a mold and high pressure is applied so that the metal can be pushed into the exact shape required. Hydroforming a component in this way means that several different operations such as stamping** and welding are no longer required. Hydroforming is used where there is demand for lower weight with high strength.

[注] hydroforming*：ハイドロフォーミング（液圧成形）　stamping**：スタンピング（打ち抜き加工）

(b) There are few affordable ways for medical students to practice surgery. Virtual-reality (VR) simulators will help, but they still have one problem: students cannot touch the actual environment in a meaningful way. A company developed a new VR surgical simulator to solve this problem. They incorporated haptic* feedback so that doctors can "feel" their actions as if they were really performing surgery. This new simulator costs as little as \$8,000, which is far less than traditional systems.

[注] haptic*：触覚の

Ⅵ　次の (a) から (c) より 2 問選び、英訳しなさい。なお、選んだ 2 問の記号を解答欄の□に記入しなさい。□の記入がない場合は減点の対象になります。

(a) この掃除機は、長年にわたって優れた性能を発揮するように設計されております。定期点検を受けていただくと、長期的に見てコストパフォーマンスが高まります。保証対象外の製品につきましては、サービスエンジニアが無料で修理査定を行います。

(b) プレートテクトニクス * は、地球の表面を形成する岩の層の動きを説明する理論だ。1960 年代に打ち立てられたこの理論は、造山の過程や火山、地震や地球の表面の進化を理解するための統一的背景 ** を提供することにより、地球科学に大きな変化をもたらした。

[注] プレートテクトニクス * : plate tectonics　　統一的背景 ** : uniform context

(c) コロイド * は、溶解や懸濁 ** はせず、液体中に分散する *** 物質である。コロイドは、原子や通常の分子よりも大きいが、肉眼で見るには小さすぎる粒子で構成されている。コロイドの例として、牛乳、澱粉、インクなどがある。

[注] コロイド * : colloid　…を懸濁する ** : suspend　…を分散させる *** : disperse

第 125 回 (2021.1)

I　次の (a) から (e) の語に、それぞれ相当する記述を選び、その番号を解答欄に記入しなさい。

(a) brew
- 1. inhale and exhale air using the lungs
- 2. cook meat by direct radiant heat over a grill
- 3. make beer from malt and other ingredients

(b) plateau
- 1. an area of high or mountainous land
- 2. a large area of high and fairly flat land
- 3. an area of low-lying, wet and muddy land

(c) equation
- 1. a mathematical statement that shows two amounts are the same
- 2. a mathematical expression of a general fact or rule in letters and symbols
- 3. a mathematical formula that shows exponential growth

(d) benign
- 1. tending to produce death or deterioration
- 2. mild character of an illness that does not cause death
- 3. persisting or constantly recurring character of an illness

(e) bisect
- 1. not leaning to one side or the other but exactly vertical
- 2. a number that cannot be divided exactly by two
- 3. to divide something into two equal parts

Ⅱ　次の (a)、(b)、(c) の英文の ( ) に入れる最適な語を下の 1 から 12 より選び、その番号を解答欄に記入しなさい。なお、 1 から 12 は 1 回しか使えない。

(a) DNA is the (a-1) material in humans and almost all other organisms. It is generally (a-2) in the nucleus of a cell but also in the mitochondria.

(b) A cleanroom is an environment (b-1) which the concentration of airborne particles (b-2) dust and chemical vapor is controlled.

(c) When the brakes are applied, it (c-1) the brake pads to press against the brake rotor, (c-2) the necessary friction to stop the vehicle.

1. on	2. excluded	3. inorganic	4. in
5. including	6. hereditary	7. generating	8. absorbed
9. obtains	10. causes	11. prevents	12. found

Ⅲ　次の (a) から (e) のそれぞれの英文を情報を変えずに最も簡潔に書き直した英文を 1 つ選び、その番号を解答欄に記入しなさい。

(a) Changes to the structure of chromosomes can have an adverse effect that can cause problems with the function of the body's systems.

　　1. Changing the structure of chromosomes is harmful to the body's systems.
　　2. Changes to the structure of chromosomes can adversely affect the body's systems.
　　3. Changes to the chromosome structure are adversely problematic because of the body's systems.

(b) Even if a shape-memory wire is bent and deformed, the wire "remembers" and returns to its originally designed shape.

  1. A shape-memory wire returns to its original shape before it is bent and deformed.
  2. Bend or deform the shape-memory wire; otherwise its original shape will not be restored.
  3. A shape-memory wire returns to its pre-determined shape even if you bend or deform it.

(c) Products made from soybeans are often used as an alternative to those made from milk because they do not contain lactose.

  1. Lactose-free products made from milk are alternated by soy products.
  2. Lactose-free soy products are often used as an alternative to dairy products.
  3. Dairy products do not contain lactose like soy products do because they are made from milk.

(d) A high fever, and a rash that follows the fever, are symptoms of measles.

  1. Symptoms of measles are a rash followed by a high fever.
  2. A high fever of measles is a symptom of a rash.
  3. Symptoms of measles include a high fever followed by a rash.

(e) The elements on the periodic table that are classified as metals make up more than two thirds of the table.

  1. More than one-third of the elements on the periodic table are classified as non-metals.
  2. Metals constitute over two-thirds of the elements on the periodic table.
  3. Metals making up more than two-thirds of the periodic table are classified as elements.

Ⅳ　次の (a) から (d) の各組の英文が同じ意味になるように、（　　　）に
　　入れる最適な語を下の 1 から 12 より選び、その番号を解答欄に記入し
　　なさい。なお、1 から 12 は 1 回しか使えない。文頭に来るべき語であっ
　　ても先頭は小文字になっている。

(a)　The thing that makes humans different from all other mammals
　　　is the fact that we talk with each other.

　　　(　　　　) makes humans different from all other mammals is
　　　that we talk with each other.

(b)　Ensure that the sensor is mounted at an angle of 90 degrees to
　　　the base plate.

　　　Ensure that the sensor is mounted (　　　　) to the base
　　　plate.

(c)　Many insects help break down dead plants and wildlife into
　　　simpler constituents.

　　　Many insects help (　　　) dead plants and wildlife.

(d)　The connecting valve must be securely tightened so as not to
　　　cause a water leak.

　　　The connecting valve must be securely tightened so (　　　　)
　　　water will not leak.

1. dismantle　　2. it　　　　　3. proportional　4. perpendicular
5. what　　　　6. if　　　　　7. that　　　　　8. fact
9. decompose　 10. parallel　　11. decline　　　 12. and

63

V　次の (a)、(b) より 1 問選び、和訳しなさい。なお、選んだ 1 問の記号を解答欄の□に記入しなさい。□の記入がない場合は減点の対象になります。

(a) Newton's Third Law of Motion, the law of action and reaction, states that when a force acts upon an object, an equal and opposite force is applied at the same time. In simpler terms, when something pushes an object, the object pushes back with equal force. When a car's engine starts and makes its wheels spin, its wheels push against the road, and the road applies the opposing force, which enables the car to move forward.

(b) The term pH is a numerical value from 0 to 14 indicating the concentration of hydrogen ions and hydroxide ions*. At a value of 7, the concentrations of both ions are equal and the solution is neutral. Below 7, a liquid is acidic, with the hydrogen ion concentration increasing as the pH value falls from 7 to 0. Above 7, a liquid is alkaline, with the hydroxide ion concentration increasing as the pH value increases.

［注］hydroxide ion*：水酸化物イオン

VI 次の (a) から (c) より 2 問選び、英訳しなさい。なお、選んだ 2 問の
　　記号を解答欄の□に記入しなさい。□の記入がない場合は減点の対象
　　になります。

(a) 太陽は、電子や陽子*などの荷電粒子**を含む太陽風を作り出し
　　ている。これらの粒子は、自らの持つ高い運動エネルギーと、宇
　　宙に広がる大気圧プラズマの一種である太陽コロナの高い温度に
　　よって、太陽の強い重力から解き放たれる。
　　[注] 陽子*: proton　　荷電粒子**: charged particle

(b) G-Cans プロジェクトで知られる首都圏外郭放水路*は、深さ
　　50m、長さ 6.5km のコンクリートの地下水路システムである。こ
　　の巨大構造物の建設は、1992 年から 2006 年の 14 年間をかけて
　　成し遂げられた。年間 7 回ほど、豪雨の際に水を迂回させ、東京
　　の街路が急流の川に変わるのを防いでいる。
　　[注] 首都圏外郭放水路*: The Metropolitan Area Outer Underground Discharge
　　Channel

(c) 哺乳類とは、皮膚が毛で覆われている温血*動物のことを言う。
　　一般に、雌の哺乳動物は、卵を産むのではなく子供を産み、自分
　　の体から分泌された**ミルクを幼い子供に与える。クジラやアザ
　　ラシ***などの哺乳類は海に住んでいるが、馬、猿、ヒトなどの
　　哺乳類は陸上に住んでいる。
　　[注] 温血の*: warm-blooded　　…を分泌する**: secrete　　アザラシ***: seals

第 124 回 (2020. 11)

I　次の (a) から (e) の語に、それぞれ相当する記述を選び、その番号を解答欄に記入しなさい。

(a) transverse
　　1. changing the appearance or form
　　2. crossing from side to side
　　3. lasting only a short period of time

(b) residue
　　1. a small amount of something that remains at the end of a process
　　2. a person who lives permanently in a specified area
　　3. a substance used to cover and protect a surface

(c) subsequent
　　1. characterized by regular sequence of parts
　　2. beneath the surface of the water
　　3. occurring or coming later or after

(d) hub
　　1. a device for keeping two parts of an electric circuit in contact
　　2. the act of moving a part of a machine so that it fits another part
　　3. a common connection point of devices in a network

(e) base
　　1. a chemical substance that combines with an acid to form a salt
　　2. a white powder that can be mixed with water and used as a medicine
　　3. a substance used for treating illness

Ⅱ　次の (a)、(b)、(c) の英文の（　）に入れる最も適切な語を下の 1 か
　　ら 12 より選び、その番号を解答欄に記入しなさい。なお、1 から 12
　　は 1 回しか使えない。

(a) In meteorology, a cyclone is a large-scale air mass that (　a-1　)
　　around a strong center of low atmospheric (　a-2　).

(b) An abbreviation is typically a shortened form of words, such as
　　Dr., (　b-1　) an (　b-2　) contains a set of initial from a phrase, such
　　as LED.

(c) In 1869, Mendeleev discovered that elements with similar (　c-1　)
　　appear periodically while he was (　c-2　) 63 elements in order of
　　increasing atomic numbers.

1. when	2. responses	3. pressure	4. properties
5. whereas	6. rotates	7. temperature	8. measuring
9. antonym	10. acronym	11. arranging	12. reciprocates

Ⅲ　次の (a) から (e) のそれぞれの英文を情報を変えずに最も簡潔に書き
　　直した英文を 1 つ選び、その番号を解答欄に記入しなさい。

(a) When the air in the container is removed, the ringing clock in the
　　container sounds fainter and fainter until you can barely hear it.

　　1. When there is no air in the container, you can faint hearing the
　　　　clock sound from the container.
　　2. When the air in the container is removed, the clock in the
　　　　container stops ringing.
　　3. When the container is vacuumized, the ringing clock sound
　　　　from the container dies away.

(b) Water and oil are immiscible but they can be mixed in the presence of soap.

　1. Water and oil emulsify soap.

　2. Water and oil do not mix but soap makes it possible.

　3. Water is immiscible with oil because of soap.

(c) Herbal supplements are used by people for the maintenance or improvement of their health.

　1. People use herbal supplements to maintain or improve their health.

　2. Herbal supplements used to maintain or improve people's health.

　3. Herbal supplements use maintenance or improvement of people's health.

(d) In many cases, it is common for some materials to be wasted during the manufacture of a product.

　1. The waste of materials is usually occurred during manufacturing.

　2. During manufacturing, materials are often wasted.

　3. During the manufacturing, material waste was commonly occurring.

(e) A gear is a wheel that has teeth that are located at even intervals around its circumference.

　1. A gear is a wheel with teeth set evenly around its circumference.

　2. A gear has a circumference with a wheel that has teeth.

　3. A wheel has a gear located around the gear's circumference.

Ⅳ　次の (a) から (d) の各組の英文が同じ意味になるように、（　）に入れ
　　る最も適切な語を下の 1 から 12 より選び、その番号を解答欄に記入し
　　なさい。なお、1 から 12 は 1 回しか使えない。文頭に来るべき語であっ
　　ても先頭は小文字になっている。

(a)　Transistors were used in every place where amplification was
　　　required in a tight space.

　　　Transistors were used (　　　　) space-efficient amplification
　　　was required.

(b)　In spite of the fact that "fire ice" is another name for methane
　　　hydrate, it is not ice in the physical sense.

　　　(　　　　) methane hydrate is called "fire ice," it is not ice in the
　　　physical sense.

(c)　Ensure that a password is set for your user account to keep
　　　people from accessing your computer without permission.

　　　Ensure that a password is set for your user account to prevent
　　　(　　　　) access to your computer.

(d)　Oxygen makes up about 20% of the air in the earth's
　　　atmosphere.

　　　About (　　　　) of the air in the earth's atmosphere is oxygen.

1.　one-fifth　　2.　which　　3.　anonymous　　4.　when

5.　restricted　　6.　a quarter　　7.　if　　8.　unauthorized

9.　although　　10. whatever　　11. wherever　　12. five to one

V　次の (a)、(b) より 1 問選び、和訳しなさい。なお、選んだ 1 問の記号を解答欄の□に記入しなさい。□の記入がない場合は減点の対象になります。

(a) Everyone's eyes contain a natural chemical called melanin within the iris*. The more melanin someone's eyes contain, the darker the color will be. Some people have made assumptions that eye color may make a difference to the way people actually see things. The truth is, while eye color does not affect how people see something, it can cause them to have different sight abilities in various lighting conditions. The melanin concentration in the pigment** of the iris cells acts as a way to protect the iris from strong sunlight.

［注］iris*: 虹彩　　pigment**: 色素

(b) Attempts to develop rechargeable lithium-metal batteries failed due to safety problems. Because of the inherent instability of lithium metal, especially during charging, research shifted to a non-metallic lithium battery using lithium ions. Although slightly lower in energy density than lithium-metal batteries, lithium-ion batteries are safe, provided that certain precautions are taken during charging and discharging. The energy density of lithium-ion batteries is typically twice that of standard nickel-cadmium batteries. Lithium-ion batteries have potential for higher energy densities.

Ⅵ　次の (a) から (c) より 2 問選び、英訳しなさい。なお、選んだ 2 問の
　　記号を解答欄の□に記入しなさい。□の記入がない場合は減点の対象
　　になります。

(a) 運輸活動 * は、米国では最大の、そして世界では 4 番目に大きな温
　　室効果ガス ** の排出源である。そのため、よりクリーンな車両や
　　大量輸送システムへ大きく舵を切らなければ、危険レベルの地球
　　温暖化を回避するために必要な排出削減の達成はありえない。
　　［注］運輸活動 *: transportation　　　温室効果ガス **: greenhouse gas

(b) 質量は、物理学においては、慣性 * の量的な尺度 ** であり、すべ
　　ての物質の基本的特性である。質量は、力が加えられた際に、速
　　度や位置の変化に対し物体が示す抵抗のことである。物体の質量
　　が大きければ大きいほど、加えた力による変化は小さくなる。
　　［注］慣性 *: inertia　　尺度 **: measure

(c) 全ての気象変化は、大気の様々な場所における温度変化が原因だ。
　　地球に向かって放射された * 太陽エネルギーは、私たちの生活や天
　　候を左右している。地球上において、赤道 ** に近い地域は、北極
　　や南極に近い地域よりも太陽からの熱を多く受ける。このように
　　地球が不均一に加熱されることにより、北風や南風が生じるのだ。
　　［注］放射する *: radiate　　赤道 **: equator

第 122 回 (2020. 1)

I 次の (a) から (e) の語に、それぞれ相当する記述を選び、その番号を解答欄に記入しなさい。

(a) classify
1. to make modern design classical
2. to divide things into groups according to common features
3. to make a subject matter suitable for a classroom

(b) contour line
1. a line joining points of equal height and indicating hills, valleys, and the steepness of slopes
2. a line indicating the course of a violent tropical storm on the weather map
3. a line joining the opposing corners of a rectangle

(c) cosmic rays
1. rays that are composed of solar rays
2. rays that are used for cosmetic purposes
3. rays that reach earth from outer space

(d) fertilizer
1. a chemical substance which farmers put on their crops to kill harmful insects
2. a chemical substance added to soil to increase its fertility
3. a chemical substance that kills or inhibits the growth of harmful microorganisms

(e) amplify
1. to increase something, such as the volume of sound
2. to make more than enough
3. to regulate the voltage on an electronic circuit

Ⅱ 次の (a)、(b)、(c) の英文の ( ) に入れる最適な語を下の 1 から 12 より選び、その番号を解答欄に記入しなさい。なお、1 から 12 は 1 回しか使えない。

(a) Telescopes captured visible, infrared, and ultraviolet (a-1), followed (a-2) X-rays and radio waves days later.

(b) Centrifugal force is an outward (b-1) force that is exerted when a body of mass rotates (b-2) an axis.

(c) A diet low in calcium can contribute to decreased bone (c-1) and have a negative (c-2) on overall bone health.

1. by	2. external	3. potential	4. in
5. impact	6. dislocation	7. light	8. about
9. radial	10. beam	11. of	12. density

Ⅲ 次の (a) から (e) のそれぞれの英文を情報を変えずに最も簡潔に書き直した英文を 1 つ選び、その番号を解答欄に記入しなさい。

(a) Aeronautics is a field of study involved with the design and manufacture of air flight capable machines.

1. Aeronautics are the capability of air flight machines that can design and manufacture.
2. Aeronautics is studied, designed and manufactured in air flight capable machines.
3. Aeronautics is the study of design and manufacture of aircraft.

(b) According to a famous equation, mass and energy are the same physical entity and can be changed into each other.

1. A famous equation states that mass and energy are interchangeable if they are physical.
2. A famous equation states that mass and energy are essentially the same, and are interchangeable.
3. A famous physician found out that mass equates energy, and that they are entirely changed into each other.

(c) The job of a car suspension system is to maximize the friction between the tires and the road surface, and to provide steering stability with good handling.

1. A car suspension system's friction is maximized between the tires and road, so the steering becomes stable and handles well.
2. A car suspension system maximizes the friction of the tires and the road with its stability and good handling.
3. A car suspension system maximizes tire-road friction, and makes the car stable and handle well.

(d) Most plants make their own food by producing substances they need by combining other substances, but fungi cannot do so.

1. Fungi cannot synthesize their own food like most plants do.
2. Fungi cannot reproduce their own nutrition like most plants do.
3. Most plants can produce other substances, but fungi cannot.

(e) The compatibility of this smartphone with Android 9 has been confirmed.

1. This smartphone supports Android 9.
2. This smartphone and Android 9 can be exchanged.
3. Android 9 can be comparable to this smartphone.

Ⅳ　次の (a) から (d) の各組の英文が同じ意味になるように、(　　　) に入れる最適な語を下の1から12より選び、その番号を解答欄に記入しなさい。なお、1から12は1回しか使えない。

(a) ┌ A chemical reaction is a process through which substances are
　　│ converted into other substances.
　　│
　　│ A chemical reaction is a process (　　　) converts substances
　　└ into other substances.

(b) ┌ By using this method, we will be able to save more money and
　　│ energy.
　　│
　　└ This method (　　　) us to save more money and energy.

(c) ┌ You have to put the system back to the default.
　　│
　　└ The system has to be (　　　).

(d) ┌ This plastic tray can be naturally decomposed by the action of
　　│ bacteria.
　　│
　　└ This plastic tray is (　　　).

1. provides 　　 2. digestible 　 3. organized 　 4. initialized

5. where 　　　 6. minimized 　 7. that 　　　 8. makes

9. biodegradable 　 10. allows 　　 11. what 　　 12. transparent

Ⅴ　次の (a) から (d) より２問選び、和訳しなさい。なお、選んだ２問の
記号を解答欄の□に記入しなさい。

(a) Methane hydrate is a crystalline solid that consists of a methane
molecule surrounded by a cage of interlocking water molecules.

(b) Living organisms, including humans, have an internal, biological
clock that helps them anticipate and adapt to the regular rhythm of
the day.

(c) Friction is the force of resistance when two surfaces slide against
each other. Frictional resistance is measured as the coefficient of
friction.

(d) Do not use this device in places where the temperature is
extremely high or low, or in places exposed to direct sunlight.

Ⅵ　次の (a)、(b) より１問選び、その下線部を和訳しなさい。なお、選ん
だ１問の記号を解答欄の□に記入しなさい。

(a) The turbocharger is bolted to the exhaust manifold of the engine.
The exhaust from the cylinders spins the turbine, which works
like a gas turbine engine. (1) The turbine is connected by a shaft
to the compressor, which is located between the air filter and the
intake manifold*. The compressor pressurizes the air going into
the cylinders. (2) The exhaust from the cylinders passes through
the turbine blades, causing the turbine to spin. The more the
exhaust that goes through the blades, the faster they spin.
［注］intake manifold* : 吸気マニホールド

(b) Genes are the basic units of all life on earth. They are responsible for the characteristics of organisms. Not all groups of animals have the same degree of genetic diversity. (1) Kangaroos, for example, come from relatively recent evolutionary lines and are genetically very similar. Carnivorous marsupials, called dasyurids*, come from more ancient lines and are genetically far more diverse. (2) Some scientists believe that we should concentrate on saving more genetically diverse groups, such as dasyurids, which include the Tasmanian devil, the numbat and the quoll.

［注］dasyurids*: フクロネコ科

Ⅶ 次の (a)、(b)、(c) より 2 問選び、その下線部を英訳しなさい。なお、選んだ 2 問の記号を解答欄の□に記入しなさい。

(a) 免疫系は人間の体を病気から守ってくれる一方、自分自身の組織は攻撃しないよう自己防衛機能を持っている。一部のがんはこの「ブレーキ」を悪用し、免疫システムの攻撃を逃れることができる。アリソン教授と本庶教授は、このブレーキを動かすたんぱく質を阻害することで、免疫システムによるがん攻撃を可能にする方法を発見した。この発見により新薬が開発され、以前は治療できないとされていた進行がん*患者の希望となっている。

［注］進行がん*: advanced cancer

(b) 光は、波のように進む。この波について説明するために、科学者たちは波長という概念を用いる。長い波長*を有する光波**もあれば、短い波長を有する光波もある。波長が異なれば、異なる色として現れる。例えば、波長の長い光は赤く見え、波長の短い光は紫に見える。太陽光はすべての波長、つまり色を含むが、すべて混ざっているので白い光として見える。

［注］波長*: wavelengths　　光波**: light waves

(c) 化学反応は原子同士が互いに結合したり、分かれたりする場合に生じる。化学反応に加わる物質は反応物質*といわれ、反応の最後の段階で生成される物質は生成物**と言われる。反応物質と生成物との間には矢印が引かれて化学反応の方向が示されるが、化学反応は必ずしも一方向のみ発生するわけではなく、双方向に発生する場合もある。

［注］反応物質*: reactant　　生成物**: product

第 121 回 (2019. 11)

I　次の (a) から (e) の語に、それぞれ相当する記述を選び、その番号を解答欄に記入しなさい。

(a) free electron
  1. any electron consisting of a proton and a neutron
  2. any electron not attached to an ion, atom, or molecule
  3. any electron radiated from the nucleus of an atom

(b) forge
  1. to shape a metal by pouring it into a mold
  2. to make a metal object thinner and weaker by beating it
  3. to shape a metal object by heating and beating it

(c) metal fatigue
  1. a weakness that develops in metal structures that are used repeatedly
  2. the ability to resist being scratched
  3. the ability to be stretched and to return to its original shape

(d) metabolism
  1. the process of digesting food
  2. the construction of complex chemical compounds from simpler ones
  3. the chemical processes that occur within a living organism in order to maintain life

(e) elastic
  1. capable of recovering size and shape after deformation
  2. easily broken or damaged
  3. easy to mold, cut, compress, or fold; not hard or firm to the touch

II　次の (a)、(b)、(c) の英文の (　) に入れる最も適切な語を下の 1 から 12 より選び、その番号を解答欄に記入しなさい。なお、1 から 12 は 1 回しか使えない。

(a) The nanoscale—the world (　a-1　) atoms, molecules, proteins, and cells rule the roost—is a place where science and technology (　a-2　) an entirely new meaning.

(b) Newly fabricated super strong lumber is created by (　b-1　) a wood block (　b-2　) a water-based solution of sodium hydroxide and sodium sulfite.

(c) The Doppler (　c-1　) can be observed when the source of the sound is moving (　c-2　) to the observer.

1. lose	2. which	3. in	4. close
5. of	6. where	7. affect	8. gain
9. boiling	10. relative	11. effect	12. drying

III　次の (a) から (e) のそれぞれの英文を情報を変えずに最も簡潔に書き直した英文を 1 つ選び、その番号を解答欄に記入しなさい。

(a) The rotor of a wind turbine is connected to the main shaft, which spins a generator to create electricity.

1. A wind turbine creates electricity by spinning the rotor first, then the main shaft.
2. A wind turbine's rotor is spun by the electricity from a generator through the main shaft.
3. A wind turbine's rotor turns an electric generator via its main shaft.

(b) A rainbow is a meteorological phenomenon in which sunlight is refracted by way of drops of water in the atmosphere.

   1. A rainbow is a meteorological phenomenon where sunlight is refracted by water drops in the atmosphere.

   2. A rainbow is a meteorological phenomenon that reflects sunlight along water drops in the atmosphere.

   3. A rainbow is a meteorological phenomenon of sunlight refraction through drops in atmospheric water.

(c) When water vapor in the atmosphere are changed to a liquid, water droplets are formed.

   1. Water droplets form when atmospheric water vapor condenses.

   2. Water droplets are formed because the air is changed to a liquid.

   3. Atmospheric water vapor is the cause of water droplets.

(d) A cuboid is a box-shaped object whose six sides are all flat and whose angles are all right angles.

   1. A cuboid has six rectangular faces at right angles to each other.

   2. A cuboid is bounded by six equal squares at right angles each other.

   3. A cuboid is a hexahedron with six faces at any angles to each other.

(e) Under the new regulation, there is a limit to the amount of greenhouse gases that can be emitted from vehicles.

   1. There is a new regulation that shows the way to reduce exhaust gas amount.

   2. The new regulation limits greenhouse gas emissions from vehicles.

   3. The new regulation raised an issue on the effect of greenhouse gases.

Ⅳ　次の (a) から (d) の各組の英文が同じ意味になるように、( ) に入れ
　　る最も適切な語を下の 1 から 12 より選び、その番号を解答欄に記入し
　　なさい。なお、1 から 12 は 1 回しか使えない。

(a)　The newly developed engine can save fuel by 10% compared
　　　with the previous design.

　　　The newly developed engine is 10% more ( ) than the
　　　previous design.

(b)　A mixture is a physical combination of pure substances; it has
　　　no definite or fixed composition.

　　　A mixture is a physical combination of pure substances ( )
　　　any definite or fixed composition.

(c)　Some mushrooms that you can eat are similar in appearance to
　　　poisonous species.

　　　Some ( ) mushrooms have similar appearances to
　　　poisonous species.

(d)　Confidential data should not be sent via e-mail unless converted
　　　into a secret code.

　　　Confidential data should not be sent via e-mail unless ( ).

1.　except　　2.　fuel-dependent　3.　classified　　4.　edible

5.　delicious　6.　fuel-efficient　　7.　fuel-consumption　8.　encrypted

9.　decoded　10. of　　　　　　　11. without　　　　12. feasible

Ⅴ　次の (a) から (d) より 2 問選び、和訳しなさい。なお、選んだ 2 問の
　　記号を解答欄の□に記入しなさい。

(a) Using these Boolean operators can greatly reduce or expand the
number of records returned.

(b) Conduction allows heat to spread throughout a material and possibly
into a different material that is in contact with the hot material.

(c) The most common bond in organic molecules is a covalent bond*
that involves the sharing of electrons between two atoms.
[注] covalent bond *: 共有結合

(d) The viscosity of a liquid decreases as the temperature rises,
whereas the viscosity of air increases with temperature.

Ⅵ　次の (a)、(b) より 1 問選び、その下線部を和訳しなさい。なお、選ん
　　だ 1 問の記号を解答欄の□に記入しなさい。

(a) Inside your ear is a very thin piece of skin called the eardrum. (1)
When your eardrum vibrates, your brain interprets the vibrations
as sound—that's how you hear. (2) Rapid changes in air pressure
are the most common thing to vibrate your eardrum. When
something vibrates, it moves the air particles around it. Those air
particles in turn move the air particles around them, carrying the
pulse of the vibration through the air as a traveling disturbance.

(b) (1) <u>Development in artificial intelligence and robotics will make it possible to operate many drones at the same time.</u> (2) <u>Some transportation companies are designing helicopter-sized versions that could carry people around like flying taxies without a pilot on board.</u> Like it or not, the sky is about to become far busier.

Ⅶ　次の (a)、(b)、(c) より2問選び、その下線部を英訳しなさい。なお、選んだ2問の記号を解答欄の□に記入しなさい。

(a) 海の生き物に必要な栄養は、まず、海の表層にいる植物プランクトン（phytoplankton）が、太陽の光を受けて光合成で作りだす。それを小さな動物プランクトン（zooplankton）がえさにして、さらに魚などが、その動物プランクトンを食べる。<u>動物プランクトンが、植物プランクトンと間違えてマイクロプラスチックを食べていることが、最近の研究でわかった。</u>

(b) エンジンはガソリンに蓄えられたエネルギーを爆発的に開放することでパワーを生み出すが、エンジンが効率的に動作するのは、シリンダー内のピストンが高速で上下運動している場合である。<u>車が単に道路沿いでアイドリングしている場合ですら、ピストンは毎分1,000回程度、上下に動く必要がある。</u>つまりエンジンが動き続けるためには最低でも毎分1,000の回転が必要になるということである。

(c) 石鹸とは、油脂と苛性ソーダとの間の化学反応の結果できるものである。石鹸の作り方には様々な方法があるが、必要な材料や道具は多くなく、基本を理解すれば、すぐにでも始めることができる。<u>しかしながら、材料の中には危険となり得る化学物質もあるため、石鹸作りの際には注意深く計量を行う必要がある。</u>

第 120 回 (2019. 7)

I　次の (a) から (e) の語に、それぞれ相当する記述を選び、その番号を解答欄に記入しなさい。

(a) quantum
1. the basic character or nature of something
2. the smallest quantity of a certain physical property
3. a very bright object in space that is similar to a star

(b) disperse
1. to make something spread over a wide area
2. to make something cease to be visible
3. to soak up a liquid substance from the surrounding area

(c) fastener
1. a mechanical device used to separate things
2. a device used to make something happen faster
3. a device used to join two or more objects together

(d) hypothesis
1. a possible, unproved explanation that is based on known facts
2. an idea that has been proved to be correct
3. an explanation for something based on memory

(e) cross section
1. an imaginary line through the center of gravity of an object
2. a picture that uses lines or curves to show the relationship between quantities
3. a drawing that shows the inside of something

Ⅱ 次の (a)、(b)、(c) の英文の ( ) に入れる最適な語を下の1から12
より選び、その番号を解答欄に記入しなさい。なお、1から12は1回
しか使えない。

(a) A fuel cell is a device that converts chemical (a-1) energy
(energy stored in molecular bonds) into (a-2) energy.

(b) Drugs are chemical (b-1) that (b-2) the nervous system and
change some function of the body or mind.

(c) Lycopene is (c-1) in many fruits and vegetables (c-2) cannot
be produced by the human body.

1. electrical	2. kinetic	3. despite	4. affect
5. dynamic	6. but	7. potential	8. consisted
9. contained	10. substances	11. effect	12. materials

Ⅲ 次の (a) から (e) のそれぞれの英文を情報を変えずに最も簡潔に書き
直した英文を1つ選び、その番号を解答欄に記入しなさい。

(a) Waxing not only makes your vehicle shiny and pretty, but it also
helps corrosive substances slide right off your paint.

   1. Waxing makes your car shiny, but corrosive substances may
   scratch the paint.
   2. Waxing makes your vehicle shiny and helps prevent corrosion.
   3. Effective and shiny waxing involves sliding it along the paint
   carefully.

(b) If there is a flaw in a blade of a turbine, the flaw can cause unstable rotation.

　　1. A flaw on a turbine blade can cause unstable rotation.

　　2. Unstable rotation can be a cause of a turbine blade flaw.

　　3. If a turbine blade is damaged, it can cause unstable rotation.

(c) If we make a close examination of hazards caused by volcanoes, we can make it possible to make their impacts become smaller.

　　1. Examining volcanic hazards can help us lessen their impacts.

　　2. Close study of volcanoes can make their impacts smaller.

　　3. Volcanic hazards and their impacts are closely examined.

(d) Direct movement of water from the surface of the ocean to the atmosphere is brought about by evaporation.

　　1. Evaporation directly enables water to move between the ocean and the atmosphere.

　　2. Water moves directly from the sea surface to the atmosphere.

　　3. Evaporation moves water directly from the ocean surface to the atmosphere.

(e) The product and its materials that do not meet the requirement of the specification shall be rejected.

　　1. The product and its materials that miss the requirement of the specification shall be rejected.

　　2. The product and its materials are failed to meet the required specification and are rejected.

　　3. The product and its materials that fail to meet the specification shall be rejected.

IV　次の (a) から (d) の各組の英文が同じ意味になるように、(　　　) に
　　入れる最適な語を下の 1 から 12 より選び、その番号を解答欄に記入し
　　なさい。なお、1 から 12 は 1 回しか使えない。

(a)　If there are acidic oxides in the atmosphere, acid rain will be
　　　produced.

　　　Acidic oxides in the atmosphere will (　　　) acid rain.

(b)　There are various useful services available through the
　　　websites of local governments.

　　　The websites of local governments (　　　) various useful
　　　services.

(c)　The system that is now used is getting old and it requires more
　　　maintenance costs.

　　　The (　　　) system is getting old, requiring more
　　　maintenance costs.

(d)　Lack of sleep can adversely affect our processes of thinking
　　　and remembering things.

　　　Lack of sleep can adversely affect our (　　　) functions.

1.　adjustment　2.　cognitive　3.　endocrine　4.　prevent
5.　predict　　　6.　result in　7.　now　　　　8.　provide
9.　issue　　　　10. cater　　　11. current　　12. recent

Ⅴ 次の (a) から (d) より2問選び、和訳しなさい。なお、選んだ2問の記号を解答欄の□に記入しなさい。

(a) Machining is the use of machines to cut pieces of material (called workpieces) and shape them into components.

(b) Protein-bound drug molecules cannot reach tissues because the protein molecules are too large to pass through the capillary fenestrations*.
[注] capillary fenestration*: 毛細血管の窓

(c) An increase in carbon dioxide concentration can make the seawater more acidic, putting marine life in danger.

(d) With the advancement of sensor and AI technologies, service robots have become increasingly popular—we use them as pets and for communication today.

Ⅵ 次の (a)、(b) より1問選び、その下線部を和訳しなさい。なお、選んだ1問の記号を解答欄の□に記入しなさい。

(a) Modern cars are equipped with brakes on all four wheels operated by a hydraulic system. (1) A hydraulic brake circuit has fluid-filled master and slave cylinders connected by pipes. The master cylinder transmits hydraulic pressure to the slave cylinder when the pedal is pressed. (2) When you step on the brake pedal, it depresses a piston in the master cylinder, forcing the fluid to flow along the pipe.

(b) Neil Armstrong's spacesuit is being restored in the Smithsonian Institute lab. (1) <u>The outer layer of the suit is made of Teflon-coated glass fiber cloth to help protect against micrometeorites*.</u> (2) <u>The helmet is equipped with a visor that protects the astronaut's eyes from ultraviolet radiation.</u> The pressurized gloves limited dexterity, but silicone rubber in the thumb fingertips provided some sense of feel.

［注］micrometeorites *: 微小隕石

Ⅶ 次の (a)、(b)、(c) より 2 問選び、その下線部を英訳しなさい。なお、選んだ 2 問の記号を解答欄の□に記入しなさい。

(a) てこを支える点を支点、力を加える点を力点、物体に力が作用する点を作用点という。支点から力点までの長さを a、支点から作用点までの長さを b とし、力の大きさを F、物体に働く力を W とすると、a × F = b × W という関係があるときに、てこがつり合う。<u>したがって、a が b より大きければ、物体が受ける力 W は、加えた力 F よりも大きくなる。</u>

(b) ナトリウムは、アルカリ金属として知られるグループに属する化学元素である。非常に反応性が高く、他の元素と結合して、多くの有用な物質を形成する。<u>ナトリウムと他の元素の化合物、つまり組み合わせで、最も身近なものは一般的な塩である。</u>化学の世界では、元素を記号で表すことが多く、ナトリウムは「Na」と表現される。

(c) パワーツール（電動工具）の使用に際しては、安全のしおり記載の指示に従ってください。パワーツールを調整したり、付属品を交換したり、片付けたりする場合は、必ず先にプラグをコンセントから抜き、バッテリーをパワーツールから取り外してください。<u>こうした事前の安全対策を行うことで、パワーツールが誤って動き出す危険性を減らすことができます。</u>

第 119 回（2019. 5）

I 次の (a) から (e) の語に、それぞれ相当する記述を選び、その番号を解答欄に記入しなさい。

(a) leverage
   1. a rigid bar used to help move a heavy load
   2. a number showing the typical value in a set of data
   3. mechanical power gained by using a lever

(b) convex
   1. having a surface curved like the interior of a circle
   2. having a surface curved like the exterior of a circle
   3. having the shape of a cone

(c) dissipate
   1. to move from a higher to a lower place
   2. to break apart the structure of something
   3. to scatter in various directions

(d) porous
   1. having many small holes through which liquid or air may pass through
   2. a small number of holes that allow air to pass through
   3. having holes with projections that prevent fluid from flowing properly

(e) geothermal
   1. relating to the physical features of the earth
   2. relating to the heat inside the earth
   3. relating to a device that measures the temperature of the earth

Ⅱ　次の (a)、(b)、(c) の英文の（　）に入れる最適な語を下の1から12
　　より選び、その番号を解答欄に記入しなさい。なお、1から12は1回
　　しか使えない。

(a) Silicon, (　a-1　) has been and will be the dominant material in
　　the semiconductor industry, will carry us into the ultra-large-
　　scale (　a-2　) (ULSI) era.

(b) A gene (　b-1　) is a permanent alteration in the DNA sequence that
　　makes up a gene, making the sequence differ (　b-2　) what is found in
　　most people.

(c) The new material could (　c-1　) an ecofriendly alternative (　c-2　)
　　steels or alloys for constructing buildings or bridges.

1. expression	2. that	3. to	4. provide
5. which	6. choose	7. intelligent	8. mutation
9. within	10. from	11. integration	12. with

Ⅲ　次の (a) から (e) のそれぞれの英文を情報を変えずに最も簡潔に書き
　　直した英文を1つ選び、その番号を解答欄に記入しなさい。

(a) A capacitor stores electrical charge but releases the charge when
　　there is no electrical current flowing into it.

　　1. A capacitor stores electric charge, but releases the charge when
　　　 no current is flowing into it.
　　2. A capacitor stores electric charge, but it is released if no current
　　　 is flowing into it.
　　3. A capacitor stores but releases electrical charge when there is
　　　 no flowing electrical current.

(b) A substance or material that can be felt or seen by us can be ultimately divided into particles known as molecules.

　　1. We can ultimately divide a substance or material that can be felt or seen into molecular particles.

　　2. A substance or material we can feel or see can be ultimately divided into particles called molecules.

　　3. A substance or material we can feel or see can be ultimately divided into particulate matter.

(c) As ancient animal bones go through a process that makes them turn into fossils, they undergo change and become rocks.

　　1. Through fossilization, ancient animal bones change into rocks.

　　2. Processing ancient animal bones produces rocks.

　　3. Animal bones changes rocks through carbonization.

(d) Brain death is defined as the loss of all functions of the brain that cannot be recovered.

　　1. Brain death is defined as the retrievable loss of all functions of the brain.

　　2. Brain death is defined as the loss of all functions of the brain.

　　3. Brain death is defined as the irreversible loss of all functions of the brain.

(e) With regard to the lead time, there has been a cutdown by introduction of this new system.

　　1. Regarding the lead time, this new system will be introduced shortly.

　　2. If this system had been introduced, the lead time would be improved.

　　3. This new system has shortened the lead time.

IV　次の (a) から (d) の各組の英文が同じ意味になるように、(　　　) に
　　入れる最適な語を下の 1 から 12 より選び、その番号を解答欄に記入し
　　なさい。なお、1 から 12 は 1 回しか使えない。

(a)　　If the pitch is higher than a certain frequency, the sound cannot
　　　 be heard.

　　　 If the pitch (　　　　　) a certain frequency, the sound cannot be
　　　 heard.

(b)　　Exposing a picture to direct sunlight for a long time will give
　　　 damage to its color.

　　　 Exposing a picture to direct sunlight for a long time will cause
　　　 its color to (　　　　).

(c)　　The interior of a parked car can heat up regardless of the
　　　 temperature of the surrounding air.

　　　 The interior of a parked car can heat up regardless of the (　　　　　)
　　　 temperature.

(d)　　This room has curtains that will not burn easily.

　　　 This room has (　　　　) curtains.

1.　reduce　　　　2.　ambiguous　　3.　ambient　　　　4.　decline

5.　exceeds　　　 6.　enhances　　　7.　inflammable　　8.　fade

9.　combustible　10.　ambulant　　 11.　flame-retardant　12.　enforces

Ⅴ　次の (a) から (d) より 2 問選び、和訳しなさい。なお、選んだ 2 問の
記号を解答欄の□に記入しなさい。

(a) Unlike batteries, fuel cells do not need to be periodically
recharged; instead, they continue to produce electricity as long as
fuel is provided.

(b) Cells provide structure for the body, take in nutrients, convert those
nutrients into energy, and perform specialized functions.

(c) Electrical engineering deals with relatively large electric currents,
whereas electronics deals with how to control things using tiny
electric currents.

(d) Less than eleven hours after the gravitational waves appeared,
astronomers spotted a new point of visible light in the sky.

Ⅵ　次の (a)、(b) より 1 問選び、その下線部を和訳しなさい。なお、選ん
だ 1 問の記号を解答欄の□に記入しなさい。

(a) Data is transferred in a variety of forms between nodes. (1) It can
be sent in the form of analog signals, or can be converted into
digital bit streams. Typically, network data transfer between a
local computer and a remote server uses digital schemes. (2) Data
can even be sent without a network – for instance, you can copy it
to a memory device and carry the device to another location.

(b) Tropical cyclones are compact, circular storms, generally some 320 km (200 miles) in diameter, whose winds swirl around a central region of low atmospheric pressure. (1) The winds are driven by the low-pressure core and by the rotation of the earth, which deflects the path of the wind through a phenomenon known as the Coriolis force. As a result, (2) tropical cyclones rotate counterclockwise in the Northern Hemisphere and clockwise in the Southern Hemisphere.

Ⅶ 次の (a)、(b)、(c) より 2 問選び、その下線部を英訳しなさい。なお、選んだ 2 問の記号を解答欄の□に記入しなさい。

(a) 振り子は、同じ長さであれば、おもりの重さや振れる幅に関係なく、同じ時間で振れる。機械式時計のてんぷは振り子の役目をしていて、1 秒を正確に刻む。てんぷ * は、てん輪 ** とひげぜんまい *** でできている部分で、時間を正確に刻むために重要な役割をしている。中に入っているひげぜんまいが伸びたり縮んだりして、てんぷが規則正しく左右に振動する。
［注］てんぷ *: balance　てん輪 **: balance wheel　ひげぜんまい ***: balance spring

(b) 最新テクノロジーの導入によって、権力者や企業はインターネット上での私たちの行動を細部まで知ることができるようになってきた。そうした情報は、企業には高値で売買され、権力者には人々の生活の監視に使われかねない。私たちの生活のオンライン化が進めば、権力者による監視は個人のプライバシーの権利に甚大な影響を及ぼす可能性がある。

(c) 食物連鎖は、動物、植物などの生物間での捕食、被食の関係を表すものである。食物連鎖は、おおむね三角形の形で表すことができ、生物量は植物などを含む下層の方が多くなっている。多くの食物連鎖の基礎となるのは太陽光であり、光合成において重要な役割を果たし、植物を成長させている。

第 118 回（2019. 1）

Ⅰ　次の (a) から (e) の語に、それぞれ相当する記述を選び、その番号を解答欄に記入しなさい。

(a) specification
　1. a book that tells you how to do something
　2. a requirement about the necessary features in the design of something
　3. a group of files that are stored together on a computer

(b) antibody
　1. a disease in which cells increase rapidly in an uncontrolled way
　2. the smallest part of a substance that can take part in a chemical reaction
　3. a substance produced by a person's body to fight disease

(c) torque
　1. a force that causes things to drop to the ground
　2. a force that causes something to spin around a central point
　3. a force that prevents one surface from sliding easily over another surface

(d) volatile
　1. changing easily into a gas at normal temperatures
　2. quantifying an ability of a liquid to vaporize
　3. changing from a gas phase to a fluid phase

(e) vein
　1. a blood vessel conveying blood from the tissues to the heart
　2. a blood cell carrying oxygen to all parts of the body
　3. a blood reservoir used to hold a certain amount of blood

II　次の (a)、(b)、(c) の英文の（　）に入れる最適な語を下の 1 から 12 より選び、その番号を解答欄に記入しなさい。なお、1 から 12 は 1 回しか使えない。

(a) The force field is the region around an object in (　a-1　) its gravitational, electric, or magnetic effects (　a-2　) be detected.

(b) Photodetectors are semiconductor devices that electrically detect (　b-1　) signals. (　b-2　) its operating wavelength, the photodetector should have high sensitivity and high response speed.

(c) Chikyu is a scientific drilling vessel (　c-1　) for deep-sea geological research. It can drill up to 7,000 meters (　c-2　) the ocean floor.

1.　depth	2.　which	3.　analog	4.　with
5.　on	6.　must	7.　below	8.　optical
9.　at	10. constructing	11. can	12. built

III　次の (a) から (e) のそれぞれの英文を情報を変えずに最も簡潔に書き直した英文を 1 つ選び、その番号を解答欄に記入しなさい。

(a) The biological clocks in living things help them determine the timing of eating and the timing of sleeping.

　　1. The biological clocks in living things help them determine when to eat and when to sleep.
　　2. The biological clocks in living things determine when to eat and when to sleep.
　　3. The biological clocks in living things help them arrange the timing of eating and sleeping.

(b) Light shining on the solar cell produces both a current and a voltage to generate electric power.

1. The solar cell converts a current into a voltage.

2. The solar cell generates light by a current and a voltage.

3. Light incident on the solar cell is converted into electricity.

(c) An A/D converter is a device that converts input analog voltage to a digital number proportional to the magnitude of the voltage.

1. An A/D converter converts analog voltage to a digital current.

2. An A/D converter converts analog voltage to a digital value.

3. An A/D converter converts a digital number to an analog value.

(d) There is a massive red tide having occurred off the coast of southwestern Florida, and the red tide appears to be growing.

1. A massive red tide has occurred off the coast of southwestern Florida and appears to be growing.

2. A massive red tide that is occurring off the coast of southwestern Florida, appearing and growing.

3. A massive red tide appeared and grew off the coast of southwestern Florida.

(e) There are two types of cell division. One is mitosis, and the other is meiosis.

1. Two cell divisions are available, one is mitosis and another is meiosis.

2. Mitosis is one cell division and meiosis is the other.

3. There are two types of cell division: mitosis and meiosis.

Ⅳ　次の (a) から (d) の各組の英文が同じ意味になるように、(　　　) に入れる最適な語を下の 1 から 12 より選び、その番号を解答欄に記入しなさい。なお、1 から 12 は 1 回しか使えない。文頭に入るべき語であっても、先頭は小文字になっている。

(a) 　A transistor is built with three layers of different semiconductor materials that are bound together.

　　A transistor has a (　　　　　) structure; three different semiconductor materials are bound together.

(b) 　Were it not for the sun, there would be no life on the earth.

　　(　　　　　) the sun, there would be no life on the earth.

(c) 　Even if alterations in a gene are minor, there is a possibility of major evolutionary consequences.

　　Minor genetic (　　　　　) can have major evolutionary consequences.

(d) 　The prevention of environmental pollution requires compliance with legal regulations.

　　(　　　　　) legal regulations is a must for preventing environmental pollution.

1. modifiers   2. compiled   3. absence   4. stratified

5. without   6. follow   7. observing   8. experiments

9. violating   10. strained   11. mutations   12. with

99

Ⅴ　次の (a) から (d) より 2 問選び、和訳しなさい。なお、選んだ 2 問の
　　記号を解答欄の□に記入しなさい。

(a) Genetically modified crops available today include those with
a pest-resistant gene, while those with a higher nutrient content
have also been studied recently.

(b) An important factor in the design of walking robots is to control
the sequences of leg movements representing specific gait*
patterns.
[注] ＊ gait：歩行

(c) A voltage applied between the base and the emitter of a transistor
allows current to flow between the collector and the emitter.

(d) Our new chips can be produced using the same semiconductor
facilities, the same standard materials, and similar techniques to
those used to manufacture conventional computer chips.

Ⅵ　次の (a)、(b) より 1 問選び、その下線部を和訳しなさい。なお、選ん
　　だ 1 問の記号を解答欄の□に記入しなさい。

(a) (1) Volcanic landforms have evolved over time as a result of
repeated volcanic activity. Mauna Loa typifies a shield volcano,
which is a huge, gently sloping landform built up of many
eruptions of fluid lava. Mount Fuji in Japan is an entirely different
formation. (2) With its striking steep slopes built up of layers
of ash and lava, Mount Fuji is a classic stratovolcano*. Iceland
provides fine examples of volcanic plateaus, while the seafloor
around Iceland provides excellent examples of submarine volcanic
structures.
[注] ＊ stratovolcano：成層火山

(b) (1) <u>Respiratory protective masks must be used whenever it is not possible or economical to remove airborne contaminants from the air.</u> The respiratory masks generally require a tight face seal so that they can provide enough protection in the hazardous environment. (2) <u>The facial area inside the respiratory mask cannot be reached from the outside unless the face seal is broken.</u> This inaccessibility of the face may cause stress on the wearers and have a negative effect on their minds.

Ⅶ　次の (a)、(b)、(c) より2問選び、その下線部を英訳しなさい。なお、選んだ2問の記号を解答欄の□に記入しなさい。

(a) <u>従来の電話機は人間の多様な音声や音色を伝えるために設計されたアナログ装置である。</u>これらの音は、その周波数や強さが滑らかに変化する連続的な電流として、アナログ信号の形で伝えられる。オシロスコープ上では、この電流は波の形で描かれる。

(b) 地震は、岩盤が応力を受けて割れることにより引き起こされる揺れである。地震による揺れの大きさは、マグニチュード、震源地、震源の深さ、地盤の状態など、様々な要因によって決まる。<u>マグニチュードが大きいほど、地震が地滑りを誘発する可能性が高くなる。</u>海底で地震が生じると、津波が起きることがある。

(c) クラゲは刺胞動物に属する。これらの生物には脳と心臓がない。心臓の役割を果たしているのは体全体だ。クラゲのフワフワとした泳ぎは、移動のためではなく、栄養分を体の隅々にまで行き渡らせるための動きである。<u>体全体が血液を体中に送るためのポンプであり、人体で言えば心臓の役目に相当する。</u>

技術英検
1級解答
ならびに工業英検準2級解答

※記述問題については模範解答を掲載しています。

第133回技術英検1級 2023.11 解答

I (a-1) 2 (a-2) 3 (b-1) 3 (b-2) 3 (c-1) 3 (c-2) 1
   (d-1) 2 (d-2) 2 (e-1) 1 (e-2) 3   30点

II (a) 3 (b) 1 (c) 2 (d) 3   16点

III (a) 6 (b) 11 (c) 8 (d) 10 (e) 9 (f) 12 24点

IV (a) 2 (b) 3 (c) 3 (d) 3 (e) 2   30点

V

(a)	Influenza vaccines, often called flu shots, protect against the four influenza viruses.
(b)	While these activities are entirely beneficial, they do not stop the impact of carbon emissions in the atmosphere.
(c)	Various applications of this technology are being developed, including the measurement of air pollution, hydration levels, and blood alcohol content.
	<解答のポイント> ・(a) 2文の同じ主語を1文に直した文章の主語とし、間に、関係代名詞節的に挿入句で often 以降の内容が入っていれば合格点となる。模範解答のように which are を省略するとより短くなり、理想的である。 ・(b) 構文的には、while、または although を文頭に使って1文にまとめる。halt の代わりにより一般的な stop を使い、冗長的な irreversible、already present なども省略すると理想的である。 ・(c) Example of these…のところを including や such as などで結び、1文にする。

30点

VI

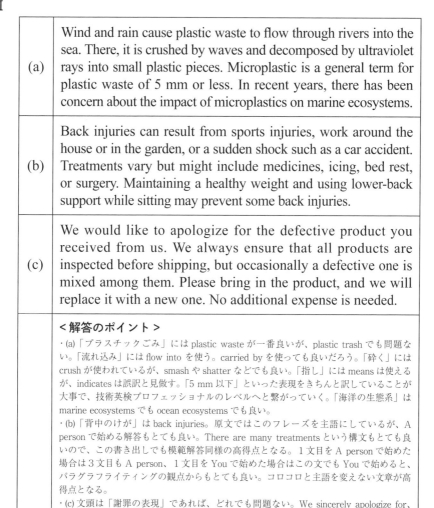

(a)	Wind and rain cause plastic waste to flow through rivers into the sea. There, it is crushed by waves and decomposed by ultraviolet rays into small plastic pieces. Microplastic is a general term for plastic waste of 5 mm or less. In recent years, there has been concern about the impact of microplastics on marine ecosystems.
(b)	Back injuries can result from sports injuries, work around the house or in the garden, or a sudden shock such as a car accident. Treatments vary but might include medicines, icing, bed rest, or surgery. Maintaining a healthy weight and using lower-back support while sitting may prevent some back injuries.
(c)	We would like to apologize for the defective product you received from us. We always ensure that all products are inspected before shipping, but occasionally a defective one is mixed among them. Please bring in the product, and we will replace it with a new one. No additional expense is needed.

＜解答のポイント＞

・(a) 「プラスチックごみ」には plastic waste が一番良いが、plastic trash でも問題ない。「流れ込み」には flow into を使う。carried by を使っても良いだろう。「砕く」には crush が使われているが、smash や shatter などでも良い。「指し」には means は使えるが、indicates は誤訳と見做す。「5 mm 以下」といった表現をきちんと訳していることが大事で、技術英検プロフェッショナルのレベルへと繋がっていく。「海洋の生態系」は marine ecosystems でも ocean ecosystems でも良い。

・(b) 「背中のけが」は back injuries。原文ではこのフレーズを主語にしているが、A person で始める解答もとても良い。There are many treatments という構文もとても良いので、この書き出しでも模範解答同様の高得点となる。1 文目を A person で始めた場合は 3 文目も A person、1 文目を You で始めた場合はこの文でも You で始めると、パラグラフライティングの観点からもとても良い。コロコロと主語を変えない文章が高得点となる。

・(c) 文頭は「謝罪の表現」であれば、どれでも問題ない。We sincerely apologize for、なども使える。単語的にはどれも 1 級としては標準的であるため、正しく訳す必要がある。「直接お持ち込みいただければ」に send は使えない。ここは「持ち込むのか」それとも「送付するのか」という、業務上重要な情報だからである。「費用」は cost でも問題ない。

70 点

第 132 回技術英検 1 級　2023. 6　解答

I　(a-1) 2　(a-2) 3　(b-1) 1　(b-2) 2　(c-1) 3　(c-2) 2
　　(d-1) 1　(d-2) 1　(e-1) 2　(e-2) 3　　　　　　　　30 点

II　(a) 2　(b) 1　(c) 3　(d) 2　　　　　　　　　　　16 点

III　(a) 6　(b) 11　(c) 9　(d) 4　(e) 3　(f) 5　　　　24 点

IV　(a) 3　(b) 2　(c) 3　(d) 1　(e) 3　　　　　　　30 点

V

(a)	We are scheduling a tour of the Hiroshima factory for our new employees, and would like to know if there are several dates convenient for you for the tour in mid-April.
(b)	This year, we may have to split the 30-plus new employees into two groups to make the tours more effective.
(c)	Please reply by the end of this month, so we can send participants the schedule early next month.
	<解答のポイント> ・全体としては、主語を（ここでは we に）統一し視点を固定することで、簡潔で分かりやすい文章を作ることができる。 ・(a) は、1 文目を Regarding…を用いた副詞句にしてもよいが、前半部分で要件（工場見学の日程設定）を示し、and でつないだ後、依頼内容（都合の確認）を示した方が読みやすい。 なお、thus 等の副詞では 2 文をつなぐことができないので要注意。 ・We are scheduling…は、現在進行形で「今まさに日程調整中」の状況であることを示す。 ・「お知らせいただければ幸いです」の丁寧表現は、would like to know…で表すとよい。 ・(b) は、「効果的に見学できるように」の部分を「見学を効果的にするために」に置き換え、副詞句 to make the tours more effective という簡潔な形にできる。 ・the 30-plus new employees を 2 文目の「〜に分けて実施する」の目的語として 1 文化する。ここで new employees は、設問 (a) で読み手と書き手の間で共有済なので、定冠詞 the を付ける。同様に tours も既出なので、the tours として関連を明示する。 ・「分ける」は split、divide、separate を使用。

・(c) は、「返信いただきたい」人はこのメールの受取人で「参加者に連絡をしたい」
のは書き手であることに注意する。
・send（送る）の代わりに inform（知らせる）を使う場合、「A に B を知らせる」は
inform A of B または inform B to A となり、SVOO の文型にはできないので注意を要
する。
・「～まで（期限）」は by…で表現する。

30点

VI

(a)	Radio waves are similar to sound and light because they propagate through space while the electric and magnetic fields oscillate. However, while sound cannot propagate without a vibrating medium such as air, radio waves can propagate even in a vacuum as in outer space. The speed of propagation is the same as that of light. If any matter exists in the path, they can pass through, reflect, or diffract.
	＜解答のポイント＞ ・文頭の「電波」は、ある事象について説明している文のため、無冠詞＋複数形で表すのがよい。 ・1文目は、関係代名詞を使って、Radio waves, which propagate through space while the electric and magnetic fields oscillate, are similar to sound and light. ・3文目の「伝播速度は光と同じで」は、比較するのは、the speed of propagation と the speed of propagation で、the speed of propagation と light ではないため、that of light のように、代名詞を使って the speed of propagation を表すのが適切。 ・3文目の「通り道に物質がある場合」は、there is 構文を避けて、文頭から情報を読み手に与える文にするとより簡潔。
(b)	If you have any questions about your ABC appliance, call the ABC Helpdesk with your serial number and details of where and when you bought it. Most questions can be solved over the phone by our trained Helpdesk staff. For online help, support videos, general tips, and information about our company, visit our website at www.ABC.com/support.
	＜解答のポイント＞ ・「製造番号」は、serial number や production number。 ・「時期」は、購入した日を表し幅を持たない date や when などの表現がよい。 ・「ほとんどのご質問」の「ほとんど」は、most。almost は副詞であり名詞を修飾することはできない。

(b)	・「解決いたします」は、最善の方法を示す意味においては solve が適当。resolve は協議により解決する、決定する、分解するといった意味である。 ・「ヘルプ」、「情報」は、ここでは不可算名詞、「スタッフ」は集合名詞、「ビデオ」や「ヒント」は可算名詞であることに注意。
	The demand for meat is rapidly expanding because of the growth in global population. If demand continues to rise at its current rate, supply may not be able to meet demand. In the middle of this trend, cultured meat is attracting worldwide attention. It is made from animal cells that have been grown in a lab. It is expected to be a sustainable food ingredient that will replace traditional meat.
(c)	**＜解答のポイント＞** ・「世界人口の増加により」は、by increasing global population とすると、「世界人口を増加することにより」と意味が変わってしまうので注意。 ・「食肉」は、meat で意味が通じる。 ・「このまま」は、前の文にある需要が急速に拡大している状態を示す表現を訳出する。 ・「細胞」は、肉に多数含まれると考えられることから、cells と複数形で訳す方が自然。 ・「食材」を food と訳す場合は不可算であることに注意。「材」の意味も訳出し a sustainable food ingredient や a sustainable food material と訳すとよりよい。 ・「に代わる」は、多様な表現がある。 例：A will replace B, B will be replaced with A, A will substitute for B, B will be substituted with/by A, A will take the place of B, A will be used instead of B ほか。

70 点

技術英検1級解答ならびに工業英検準2級解答

第131回技術英検1級　2023.1　解答

I　(a) 2　(b) 3　(c) 3　(d) 1　(e) 2　　　　　　　　20点

II　(a-1) 3　(a-2) 4　(b-1) 10　(b-2) 6　(c-1) 7　(c-2) 12　30点

III　(a) 1　(b) 3　(c) 3　(d) 2　(e) 2　　　　　　　30点

IV　(a) 11　(b) 2　(c) 8　(d) 5　　　　　　　　　　20点

V

(a)

> 音の三要素は、高さ、大きさと音色である。音の高さは、音波の周波数によって決まる。周波数が高いほど音の高さは高くなり、周波数が低いほど音の高さは低くなる。ヒトは20Hzから20,000Hzの周波数の音を聞くことができる。20Hz未満の音は超低周波音と呼ばれ、20,000Hzを超える音は超音波と呼ばれる。コウモリのような動物は、超音波を使って物体を探知し、暗闇の中を進むことができる。

＜解答のポイント＞

・pitch, loudness, tone の3語は、文脈に応じた適訳が求められる。pitch は「ピッチ」「高低」「高さ」、loudness は「大きさ」「音量」、tone は「音色」「音調」など。pitch を「音程」や「間隔」と訳すのは、この文脈では望ましくない。

・2文目の determined は「周波数が変わればピッチも変わる）という意味が取れるように訳すこと。「定義される」は誤り。

・比較級＋比較級の構文は、「～するほど、～になる」という連動のニュアンスを明確に表現すること。「周波数が高いと」「周波数が高ければ」などでは不十分。

・4文目は、「人間は、～の周波数をもつ音を聞く能力がある」ことを意味する。「人間の可聴域は～である」という書き方でも良い。with は「～で」と訳しがちだが、「～の周波数『で』音を聞くことができる」は日本語として正しくない。

・5文目は「超低周波音」「超音波」という用語の定義なので、数値表現は厳格に訳すこと。lower than は「未満」「～よりも低い」、higher than は「超」「～よりも高い」などとする。「以下」や「以上」では不正確な定義になってしまう。

(a)	・navigate their way は「（障害物をよけて）うまく通り抜ける」といった意味。「（彼らの道を）ナビゲートする」や「案内する」のような直訳では意味が取れないので、自然な日本語にする工夫が求められる。
(b)	2D と 3D の印刷プロセスは基本的に同じで、同じ場所に複数の層を重ねて何かを作り出す―2D プリンタなら画像を描き、3D プリンタなら堅固な立体を構築する。3D CAD 図面は多数の二次元の断面層に変換され、3D プリンタはそれを一層ずつ最下層から上方へと何度にも分けて印刷していく。一つの立体を構築するのに、数時間を要することもある。 **＜解答のポイント＞** ・1 文目のコロンは「具体的に何が同じか」という説明が後に続くことを表している。「つまり」などの接続詞を入れてもよい。 ・to form something – のダッシュも、後に具体的な説明が続くことを表している。「『何か』とは、2D プリンタであれば『画像』、3D プリンタであれば『立体』である」という意味。 ・picture は「写真」や「絵」ではなく、より意味が広い「画像」とするのがよい。 ・この文脈では、solid を「固体」、model を「模型」とするのは不適切。「平面画像」との対比なので、solid model は「中身の詰まった立体の型」という意味になる。「堅固な立体」や「立体モデル」などとする。 ・cross-sectional は cross-section「断面」の形容詞形。cross-sectional layer は「交差する層」ではなく「断面層」となる。 ・prints one layer at a time over and over again は「一度に一層ずつの印刷を、何度も繰り返す」という意味が明確になるように訳す。直訳だと「一度に1つの層を何度も繰り返し印刷する」としがちだが、それでは違う意味に取られやすくなる。 ・bottom は「一番下の層」「底面」としてもよいが、単に「底」とするのは日本語として違和感がある。 ・最終文の can は、文脈上、「能力」ではなく「可能性」の意味になる。「数時間でできる」ではなく、「何時間もかかる可能性がある」というニュアンスを出す。

選択1問30点

Ⅵ

(a)

The advancement of artificial perception technology is remarkable. Today, optical sensors are used to identify individuals, autonomous vehicles drive at moderate speeds on the open road, and robots roam through a building and collect empty cans.

＜解答のポイント＞

・「人工的知覚技術」の「知覚」は perception が最適。この文脈では sense や recognition も可。artificial intelligence は「人工知能」なので意味が違う。また、perceptive や sensory といった形容詞を使うと、「『人工的な』『知覚の技術』」という係り受けになってしまうので不可。「『人工的な知覚』の技術」となるよう、名詞を使う必要がある。

・最後の「できるようになっている」は、能力と言うより「定常的にそのようなことが見られる」の意。動詞を単純現在で使うだけで、その意味は十分に出る。安易に助動詞 can を使って表現するのは、「識別することがある、走ることがある」のように頻度の意味にも見えかねないので、望ましくない。能力と解釈して訳すならば、動詞 enable を使って Today, the technology enables optical sensors to identify individuals, autonomous vehicles to drive…, and robots to roam… のように表現するのがよい。

・「自律」は autonomous。automatic や self のように、意味の異なる類語が多いので注意。

・「適切な速度」は moderate や appropriate で表す。「速すぎず遅すぎず」の意味合いが出ていればよい。

・「公道を」は慣用表現の on the open road が自然。on public roads でもよい。冠詞や単複には注意。

・「を歩き回る」は、roam through や roam around がイメージに合う。walk around a building も可だが、「建物を迂回して歩く」とも読めるので戸惑いが生じる。

(b)

Global petroleum demand and greenhouse gas emissions may have already peaked in 2019. This is because the pandemic could further slow economic growth, accelerate decarbonization, and force people to continue teleworking. Energy demand could thus remain suppressed for a long time to come.

＜解答のポイント＞

・「世界の石油需要と温室効果ガス排出量」のような長いフレーズは、係り受けに注意しながら訳すこと。例えば、Global demand for petroleum and greenhouse gas emissions も間違いではないが、「石油と温室効果ガス排出量に対する世界の需要」とも読めてしまい、読者が戸惑うので良くない。

・1文目の時制表現は、なかなか難しい。「2019年という過去の時点においてすでにそうだったかもしれない（と、今考えている）」ということなので、may と完了形の組み合わせで表現するのが簡潔。意味に合わせ already を補うのも効果的。

(b)	・模範解答の could は「可能性が否定できない」の意で、「することができた」という過去の意ではない。further や continue のような「継続」を示す表現と組み合わせることで、「2019 年から今までそうだったし、この後もそれが続く可能性が否定できない」という意味合いになっている。 ・「長期的に減少する」は文脈上「今後も長期にわたって減少した状態が続く」の意なので、remain suppressed for a long time となる。「長期にわたって」と「長期的には」を間違えやすいので注意。例えば decrease in the long term では「（短期的には違うかもしれないが）長期的には減少する」となり、ニュアンスが違ってしまう。 ・for a long time は単独でも良いが、to come と組み合わせると、「今後」すなわち「未来」のニュアンスであることが明確になる。could が「過去」ではなく「今後の可能性」を表している、という意味合いがよりはっきりする。
(c)	Temperature affects matter in many ways. As matter gets hotter, its molecules move faster, and its properties change. The physical state of matter is affected by its temperature. For example, at a temperature of 0° C or below, water is a solid; above 0° C, it becomes a liquid; and at 100° C, it turns into a gas. **< 解答のポイント >** ・先頭の「温度」は不可算が最適。可算にすると 3 文目にあるように個々の温度を指す。 ・「影響を与える」は、affect で他動詞。effect（名詞形）を使って訳すと英文が冗長になるので注意。 ・2 文目の和文は主語が曖昧なので、英文で明確にする必要がある。ここでは「分子」は「物質の分子」であり、「特性」も「物質の特性」。文脈にもよるが、its といった所有格を使うか、molecules of matter と明確に書く。 ・「物質」は、「個体、液体、気体」の話をしているので matter が最適。matter は不可算。可算の substance も可。 ・「特性」は properties、characteristics。nature（もともと持っている性質のこと）や feature（注意をひく顕著な特徴のこと）は、ここでは不適切。 ・「物理的な状態」の「状態」は、次の文章で「個体、液体、気体」を挙げているので、「物質の三態」を表す state が適切。condition は不可。 ・3 文目では、「以下」「〜超える」「〜では」の数量表現を正確に書く。温度の数量表現では、前置詞は above、below、at が適切。例えば、「零下」は below zero であり、under zero とは言わない。 「0° C 以下」は 0° C or below が最適。below/under/less than 0° C は未満なので不可。 「0° C を超える」は、below に対して above 0° C が最適だが、over/exceeds も可。 「100° C では（気体に変化する）」は、at 100° C が最適。

選択 2 問各 35 点

第 130 回技術英検 1 級　2022.11　解答

Ⅰ　(a) 2　(b) 1　(c) 3　(d) 1　(e) 2 　　　　　　　　　　　20 点

Ⅱ　(a-1) 5　(a-2) 8　(b-1) 10　(b-2) 2　(c-1) 7　(c-2) 1　　30 点

Ⅲ　(a) 1　(b) 2　(c) 3　(d) 2　(e) 3 　　　　　　　　　　　30 点

Ⅳ　(a) 5　(b) 12　(c) 4　(d) 9 　　　　　　　　　　　　　20 点

Ⅴ

(a)

> ガラス板などの透明な素材を通過する光線は、素材に直角に当たった場合にのみ真っ直ぐ通過する。それ以外の場合は、素材が屈折させるため、光線の方向が変わる。角度の変化は、素材によって異なる。この違いを示すのが、素材の屈折率である。屈折率が大きいほど、方向の変化が大きくなる。光線が素材に入射すると、速度が低下する。素材内部における光の速度は、屈折率に比例して低下する。

<解答のポイント>

・現在分詞 passing の時制は、現在進行形（通過している =that is passing）ではなく、文脈より現在形（通過する =that passes）。passing から plate までが形容詞句で、主語 a ray of light を修飾している。動詞は goes straight through で第 1 文型（SV）である。

・goes に係る副詞節 if…は、ここでは仮定ではなく条件を表す。「もし〜ならば」より「〜の場合」と訳す方が適切。

・only は直後の語句に係るとは限らない。ここでは、動詞 goes ではなく if 節に係り「〜の場合のみ」と訳す。

・material は可算名詞の場合「素材」や「材料」。「材質」は厳密にいうと意味が異なる。

・at right angle は「直角（90 度）に」。ちなみに、「正しい角度」は correct (proper) angle。

・otherwise は if 節（〜の場合）に呼応し、「そうではない場合」、「それ以外の場合」を意味する。

(a)	・refract は「屈折する」。類義語の reflect「反射する」、diffract「回折する」と混同しやすいので注意すること。 ・what は先行詞を含む関係代名詞で、be 動詞 is の主語。what indicates 〜は「〜を示すもの」（= the thing that indicates…）となる。 ・「the ＋比較級〜（SV）、the ＋比較級〜（SV）」は比較の定型表現で「〜すればするほど、ますます〜」。be 動詞は省略される。 ・in proportion to… は「〜に比例して」。なお「〜に反比例して」は in inverse proportion to…。
(b)	全地球測位システム（GPS）受信機の主な機能は、ユーザが正確な地理的位置を特定できるようにすることである。正確な測位を行えるよう、高度約2万 km にある3機以上の人工衛星から別々の信号を受信するように設計されている。信号には、人工衛星の軌道や搭載された原子時計の時刻の情報が含まれている。それぞれの到達時間、すなわち発信から受信までにかかる時間を比較することで、GPS 受信機は現在地を計算する。 **＜解答のポイント＞** ・The core <u>function</u> of… <u>is to enable</u> ＋ O（目的語）＋ to 不定詞は「〜の主な機能は、O が〜できるようにすることである」が正解。 「〜の主な<u>機能</u>によって利用者は<u>〜できる</u>」のような、似ているが意味が異なるうっかり表現に注意。 ・separate signals は「分離した信号」ではなく「別々の信号」。「分離（処理）した信号」であれば separated signals となる。 ・contain は「（中身の全体を）含む」。ちなみに、include は「（中身の一部を）含む」よって「他にもある」を含意。 ・These signals contain…は無生物主語なので、「この信号<u>には</u>〜が<u>含まれている</u>」と受身的に訳すと自然な日本語になる。 ・the time of atomic clocks の time は「（個々の原子時計が示す）時刻」を指す。時刻と時間は混同されがちだが、技術用語としては「時刻」（= 時間軸上の1点）と「時間」（= 時間軸上の2点間の長さ）を明確に区別することが多い。 ・the arrival times は文脈より「到着時間（= 到着時刻）」ではなく「到達時間（= 送信から受信までの所要時間）」。複数の人工衛星から送信される信号の到達時間なので、「<u>それぞれの</u>到達時間」と訳出する。 ・the time delays between transmission and reception は、送信（発信）と受信の間の遅れ時間＝「発信から受信までにかかる時間」。 ・or は、ここでは選択の接続詞「または」ではなく、言い換え（説明の補足）なので「すなわち」と訳す。

選択1問30点

VI

<table>
<tr>
<td>(a)</td>
<td>

All living things consist of cells. All cells contain a nucleus, and the nucleus contains chromosomes. Every human has 23 pairs of chromosomes in each nucleus. Children look like their parents because the genes in the chromosomes carry biological information from parents to children.

＜解答のポイント＞

・「核」を表す英単語はいくつかあるが、細胞の「核」は nucleus（複数形は nuclei）。core は「細胞核」の意味で使われることはないので、ここでの訳語としては不適切。品詞違いの nuclear（名詞ではなく形容詞）や、意味を混同しやすい atom（原子）も、うっかり使わないように注意。

・単数形・複数形の使い分けにも注意。All cells contain a nucleus は、すべての細胞（複数形）が主語となっているが、それぞれの細胞は核を1つだけ有するので、a nucleus は単数形となる。次の the nucleus contains chromosomes は、それぞれの核には複数の染色体が含まれるので、chromosomes は複数形となる。

・「すべての細胞には〜23対の染色体がある」の一文は長いが、前半は細胞の一般的な説明で、後半はヒトに限定してより具体的な説明をしている。はっきりした意味の切れ目があるので、無理に一文でまとめようとせず、二文に分けると英文を作りやすい。

・「子が親に似る」は、look like や resemble がちょうどよい。「に」があるので to を使いたくなるが、resemble は他動詞なので resemble to は誤り。

・「遺伝子」は gene(s)。混同しやすいが、DNA はここでの訳語としては不適切。遺伝情報をもつ物質（核酸）ではあるが遺伝子ではない。

・information は不加算名詞。

</td>
</tr>
<tr>
<td>(b)</td>
<td>

Biomass power generation generates power using biomass such as plant residue as fuel. CO_2 is generated even when biomass is burned. However, plants absorb CO_2 while they grow, turning it back to biomass. Thus we can assume that the amount of CO_2 in the atmosphere does not increase and that using biomass fuel is ca rbon neutral.

＜解答のポイント＞

・「バイオマス」biomass は不加算名詞。

・「発電」は、generation, power generation, electric generation など。power や electricity だけでは不十分。

・「植物残さ等」の位置に注意。「燃料としてバイオマスを使う」を先に訳し、後から付け足すと、うっかり using biomass as fuel such as plant residue のような語順にしてしまいやすい。これでは、「植物残さ等の燃料として、バイオマスを使う」となって

</td>
</tr>
</table>

<table>
<tr><td>(b)</td><td>

しまう。

・「燃焼した場合でも」の「でも」には意味がある。単に when biomass is burned ではなく、「（他の燃料と同じように）バイオマスでも CO_2 は発生するが」という課題文のニュアンスを表現すること。

・「バイオマスに戻す」は、turning it back to biomass のように目的語 it を入れること。return to biomass のような書き方では「バイオマスに戻る」となり、文意がずれる。

・「～と考えられる」がどこに係るのか、しっかり見極めること。前半の「植物は～バイオマスに戻すので、」の部分は現象として起こる事実なので「～と考えられる」の対象に含まれず、「大気中の CO_2 の量は増加しない」の部分だけが「～と考えられる」の対象である。

・「カーボンニュートラルであるとみなすことができる」の主語に注意。課題文には主語がないので、意味を考えて補ってやることが必要。Biomass fuel の他、「バイオマス発電」biomass power generation でも可。

</td></tr>
</table>

(c)	**Frequencies of 2.4 GHz band, 5 GHz band, and 60 GHz band are allocated to wireless LAN. Most wireless LAN devices are Wi-Fi certified and bear the Wi-Fi logo. Any product with the Wi-Fi logo, including home appliances and smartphones, can be connected to wireless LANs.** **＜解答のポイント＞** ・「無線 LAN には 2.4GHz 帯、5GHz 帯および 60GHz 帯の周波数が割り当てられている」は無線 LAN を主語にして能動態で書くことができないため、受動態で書くのが適切。 ・「割り当てられている」は are allocated to がよい。are assigned to も可能。 ・「2.4GHz 帯、5GHz 帯および 60GHz 帯の周波数」は Frequency bands of 2.4 GHz, 5 GHz, and 60 GHz も可能。 ・「ほとんどの無線 LAN」の「ほとんど」は一般的な何かの大部分を表す most が適切だが、almost all も可能。Most of は特定の対象の大部分を表すため、意味が異なる。 ・「機器は Wi-Fi 認証を得ており」は、devices are Wi-Fi certified が適切。authorize「～に権限を与える」や authentication「認証（身元を証明する時の意味）」は望ましくない。 ・「Wi-Fi ロゴを与えられている」は、bear「（～を）持つ、有する」を使い bear the Wi-Fi logo がよい。devices are given the Wi-Fi logo も可能。 ・「Wi-Fi ロゴを持つ製品であれば、」は、any＋単数名詞（どんな～でも、どの～でも）を使って、Any product with the Wi-Fi logo と簡潔に表現するとよい。 ・including、such as などを使った例示「家電製品でも、スマートフォンでも」の文中の位置は、その対象「Wi-Fi ロゴを持つ製品」から離れないようにする。

選択 2 問各 35 点

第129回技術英検1級　2022.6　解答

Ⅰ　(a) 1　(b) 1　(c) 2　(d) 3　(e) 1　　　　　　　　20点

Ⅱ　(a-1) 7　(a-2) 10　(b-1) 5　(b-2) 4　(c-1) 1　(c-2) 11　30点

Ⅲ　(a) 3　(b) 2　(c) 3　(d) 1　(e) 2　　　　　　　　30点

Ⅳ　(a) 3　(b) 6　(c) 9　(d) 8　　　　　　　　　　　20点

Ⅴ

> 光ファイバケーブルは、光パルスとしてデータを伝送する。光ファイバケーブルを通る光は、長距離を移動することができる。光パルスは電磁放射の影響を受けないため、光ファイバケーブルは大量の電気的干渉がある環境に適している。光ファイバケーブルの伝送速度は、より対線の数千倍である。この伝送速度の速さは、大容量のビデオ会議やその他の双方向サービスを可能にし、コミュニケーションの可能性を広げるのに役立った。

(a) **＜解答のポイント＞**

・fiber optic cable の訳は「光ファイバケーブル」が世間で最もよく使われている。日本語と英語で語順が違う用語はよくあるので、そのようなものとして覚えておく。

・carry は「運ぶ」と訳してもよいが、対象物がデータなので「伝送する」の方が自然。

・pulses of light は「光パルス」が自然。「光振動」も可。

・them は fiber optic cables を指している。1文目に複数形の名詞が2つあるので（cables と pulses）、文意を捉えず急いで訳文を作ると誤った訳をしやすい。

・transmitted through は「～を通って伝わる」だが、「～中を伝わる」という表現もよい。

・electromagnetic radiation は「電磁放射」が適切。「電気信号は外から放射され飛び込んでくる電磁波の影響を受けやすいが、光信号はそうではない」ということだから、「放射」という言葉は読者にイメージを伝えるうえで重要。

・be suitable for は「～に適している」が適切。

・thousands of times は「数千倍」のこと。thousands が複数形なので、単に「千」で

(a)	はなく「数千」となる。複数形の times は時間ではなく「〜倍」を表すことが多い。 ・This has…helped broaden の語法に注意。broaden は「〜を広げる」という動詞。help には、後ろに動詞の原形を従えて「〜するのを助ける／〜するのに役立つ」という意味を表す用法がある。 ・この文では、large-capacity は video conferencing にかかっている。「大容量」と言えばつい「通信（communication）」にかけたくなるが、構文上そのような解釈は不可であることに注意。
(b)	血管疾患の一次予防のためのアスピリンに関して、6つの主要な無作為化試験のメタ解析が行われた。95,000人以上の被験者のうち、重篤な心血管症例が発生したのは、アスピリンを服用している被験者の0.51％、服用していない被験者の0.57％であった。これは、リスクが相対的に11％減少したことになる。一方、重篤な出血の症例については、アスピリン非服用者では0.07％であったのに対し、アスピリン服用者では0.10％に増え、リスクは相対的に43％増加した。 **＜解答のポイント＞** ・前置詞句による名詞の修飾がかなり多く、係り受けを見誤りやすい。しかし、一見複雑に見えるが、主部は A meta-analysis was conducted というシンプルなもの。「メタ解析が行われた」という日本語を軸にして、順に修飾表現を足していくと、正しい訳文を作りやすい。 ・meta-analysis は「メタ分析」または「メタ解析」がよい。「統合分析」も可。「同一対象に関する複数の調査研究を比較検討し分析すること」を意味する用語。 ・パーセンテージが示されているところの訳は、特に語順に気を付けること。例えば、「アスピリンを服用している0.51％の被験者」や「0.51％のアスピリンを服用している被験者」では、意味が全く違ってしまう。 ・event は訳しにくいが、「どのぐらいの人数が発症したか」という文脈なので、「症例」などそのニュアンスが感じられる自然な表現を当てるようにする。医学用語としては「有害事象」やカタカナのまま「イベント」とすることが多い。 ・relative は「相対的な」の意。増減を表す文脈では、大抵この意味になる。「関連性がある」ではない。 ・At the same time はタイミングというより「同じ調査の中で」と解釈した方が自然。「同時に」としてもよいが、「一方」や「また」という訳し方の方がこなれている。

選択1問30点

VI

(a)

A cleanroom is a dust-free working area with strict temperature and humidity control. It plays a critical role in the research and manufacture of electronic devices, aerospace system components, and other equipment susceptible to contamination by impurities.

＜解答のポイント＞

・和文が一文で長いので、「クリーンルームとは…のことである」で区切ると、センテンスとして読みやすくなる。

・クリーンルームは cleanroom または clean room（cleanroom の方が限定的で、望ましい）。可算名詞なので冠詞が必要で、ここでは定義文の基本パターンとして a が最適。

・「温度と湿度が厳密に管理された〜部屋」は、a…area with strict temperature and humidity control, a…area where temperature and humidity are strictly controlled。… a workplace that is strictly controlled temperature and humidity は、temperature and humidity が control の目的語でも動作主でもないので不適切。ここでの「管理」は「温度や湿度を一定に保つよう制御する」の意味なので control が望ましい。manage も可だが、control ほど一定に保つの意味は強くない。

・「電子機器や航空宇宙システム部品など、不純物による汚染の影響を受けやすい機器の研究や製造において」
such as など、例示「電子機器や航空宇宙システム部品など」の文中の位置は、その対象「（〜影響を受けやすい）機器」から離れないようにする。

・「電子機器」は、electronic devices、electronic equipment。equipment は不可算名詞。

・「〜の影響を受けやすい」は susceptible to…が最適。…is easily affected by も可能。prone to…も使えるが、prone to contamination では「汚染されやすい」という意味になってしまう。ここでは、汚染された後の結果が及ぼす影響なので prone to the effect of contamination といった「影響」の含意が必要。vulnerable to 〜 は「〜に弱い、傷つきやすい」という意味で若干ニュアンスが異なる。

(b)

When organic substances such as carbohydrates are combined with oxygen, carbon dioxide and water are produced and heat is released. It looks as if the thermal energy comes out of nowhere, but it has been transformed from other forms of energy originally contained in the organic substance.

＜解答のポイント＞

・「有機物」は、organic substances/materials。「炭水化物」は有機化合物（organic compound）ではない。organism は有機体、微生物菌のこと。object は五感で知覚し得るものなので不適切。

・「結合する」は combine が最適。connect はじかに触れてもそれぞれの個別性を失わないのでここでは不適切。bond は2つの物質を接着剤などで接合することなので不適切。

・「酸素」、「二酸化炭素」は「水」と同様、物質で不可算名詞。

·「（熱が）放出される」は、emit, release がよい。いずれも他動詞なので用法に注意すること。

·「何もないところから生まれる」は、comes out of nowhere, generated from nowhere が適切。generated from nothing、created from scratch も可能。

·「もともと持っていた」は、originally contained, originally had がよい。

·「他のエネルギー」のエネルギーは不可算名詞なので、複数形をとりたい場合は other types of energy, other forms of energy にする。

·「変換する」は、transform、convert がよい。change も可だが、意味の範囲が広く、「交換する」、「全面的に変更する」というニュアンスにも取られかねないため望ましくはない。

(c)

Space debris is an unwanted artificial object orbiting the earth. Such artificial objects include artificial satellites that have finished their operations, broken artificial satellites, the upper stages of launch rockets, and fragments generated by explosions and collisions. Currently, there are about 20,000 objects measuring 10 cm or more that are being tracked from the earth, which may hinder future space activities.

＜解答のポイント＞

·「宇宙ごみ」は不可算名詞。

·「軌道周回をしている」は、地球の軌道を周回しているので orbiting the earth。動詞の orbit は「（天体の）周囲を、軌道を描いて回る」という意味。

·「運用を終えた人工衛星」は、satellites that have finished their operation のように、今まで運用されていたがその役目を終えたということが明確であること。

·「打ち上げロケットの上段部分」は、the upper stages of launch rockets がよい。

·「爆発と衝突」は、explosions and collisions で、ここでは複数形をとる。

·「10 cm 以上の物体」

～以上は 10 cm or more が最適。more than 10 cm, over 10 cm は厳密には 10 cm を超える。10 cm long は長さのみの尺度となる。

·「2万個」は twenty thousand。数字を表す場合は thousands のように複数形にならない。

·「～の妨げになる」は、hinder（事柄の進行や人の行為を遅らせたり、止めたりして妨げる）が最適。obstruct も可能。

prevent··· は「将来の宇宙活動」自体を妨げる／封じることになる。

選択2問各35点

第128回技術英検1級　2022.1　解答

Ⅰ　(a) 3　　(b) 1　　(c) 2　　(d) 1　　(e) 2　　　　　　　　20点

Ⅱ　(a-1) 11　(a-2) 5　(b-1) 8　(b-2) 2　(c-1) 9　(c-2) 4　　30点

Ⅲ　(a) 1　　(b) 1　　(c) 3　　(d) 3　　(e) 2　　　　　　　　30点

Ⅳ　(a) 4　　(b) 5　　(c) 10　(d) 8　　　　　　　　　　　　20点

Ⅴ

(a)	大気は、地球の極端な寒暖差を和らげる役割を果たす。日中、太陽の熱が空気を通過し地表を暖めると、大気はこの熱を閉じ込める。この熱は、宇宙空間にゆっくりと逃げていくため、夜はこの効果がないときよりも暖かくなる。また、大気は、流星粒子や宇宙線、太陽や星からの放射線などの危険からも、地球の生物をある程度保護している。

<解答のポイント>
・the atmosphere は、ここでは地球をとりまく「大気」のことで「大気圏」は不適切。
・moderate は、「和らげる」「穏やかにする」ことで、「調整する」は不適切。
・heat and cold は、感覚としての暑さ、寒さで、温度の高低ではない。
・penetrate the air は、「空気を通過する」「空気を通り抜ける」という意味。
・trap は、「閉じ込める」「取り込む」が適切。
・the heat escapes slowly into space は、日中、大気によって閉じ込められた熱が自ら「逃げていく」イメージ。
into space の space は、不可算で「宇宙」「宇宙空間」という意味。
・making は使役用法なので、「閉じ込められた熱がゆっくりと逃げていくため、夜が暖かくなる」という因果関係を明確にする。
・inhabitants は文脈上、人に限らないので、「生物」「生命体」とする。
・meteor particles, cosmic rays, radiation from the sun and stars, and other hazards
「何から保護しているのか」を示す最後の項目リストは、意味のまとまりを見極めて訳すこと。意味からも「カンマが項目の区切りを示し、カンマ + and は最後の項目を示す」

という基本からも、from [meteor particles], [cosmic rays], [radiation from the sun and stars], and [other hazards] というように4つのまとまりで考えるのが適切。radiation from は the sun and stars の両方にかかるが、and other hazards にはかからない。

ラジエータは自動車のエンジンなどの冷却システムに使用されている。冷却液が熱いエンジンの周りに送り込まれて熱を吸収し、自動車に備えられたラジエータ内を流れる。自動車が走行すると風がラジエータに当たり、ラジエータや内部の冷却液を冷却する。冷却システムがないとエンジンは過熱するが、エンジンのスタート直後には熱慣性によりエンジンの過熱は起こらない。質量の大きい物質の温度を変化させるには時間がかかるのである。

＜解答のポイント＞

(b) 時系列を意識しながら訳すとスムーズに訳せる。例えば, to + 不定詞が多用されているが、自然現象を表している文なので、「～するために…する」という目的を表す用法で解釈するのは不自然。「…する結果～する」というように、結果を表す用法で解釈をして、時系列の通りに並べると訳しやすい。

・for example, in vehicle engines を「例えば」にこだわらずに「自動車のエンジンなどの」とすると自然な訳になる。

・時系列を特に意識すべきところ。「冷却液が熱いエンジン回りに送り込まれる」→「冷却液がその熱を吸収する」→「自動車に備わったラジエータ内を流れる」という順序で訳す。

・coolant は「冷媒」でも意味は合っているが、液体なので、ここでは「冷却液」が適切。あるいは「クーラント」としても良い。

・pumped around the hot engine は、(冷却液が) 熱いエンジンの周りに (ポンプで)「送り込まれて」「めぐらされて」という意味。

・ここも時系列を意識して、「自動車が動く」→「風がラジエータに当たる」→「ラジエータとその中の冷却材を冷やす」という順序で訳す。to cool the radiator and the coolant inside it を「ラジエータとラジエータ内の冷却材を冷やすために風を当てる」は不適切。it は、ラジエータのこと。

・to cool は、the radiator と the coolant inside it の両方にかかる。

・this は overheat のことなので、前文とつなげても意味的に問題はない。一文にした方が、日本語表現がスムーズになり、訳しやすい。

・セミコロンは「今言ったことは、こういうことだ / こういうことだからだ」というような論理的なつながりを表している。このニュアンスが感じ取れる訳文になっているとよい。

選択1問30点

123

VI

(a)

Data science is changing our world in areas ranging from scientific discoveries to business intelligence. Tremendous opportunities are being created through combination of remarkable changes such as the digitization of information, the proliferation of sensors, breakthroughs in machine learning and visualization, and dramatic improvements in costs, bandwidth, and scalability.

＜解答のポイント＞

・「変えつつある」は単純な現在進行形が合う。現在完了進行形を使うと「これまでずっと、そして今も」という、この文脈には不要なニュアンスが出る。

・「…から…まで」を from/to で表し、「変えつつある」の change の近辺に配置してしまうと、「…から…へ変えつつある」と解釈される英文になりやすい。英語として間違いではないが、読者の誤解を招かない工夫をすることが望ましい。

・「デジタル化」は digitalization も可だが、digitization が好ましい。digitalization は「社会・生活のデジタル化」では使われるが、「情報のデジタル化」は digitization の方が自然。また、digitalization は医療関係では昔から「ジギタリス投与」の意で使われており、避けた方が無難。

・「チャンス」はここでは「機会」の意なので、opportunities とするのがよい。カタカナの音に近い chances を使うこともできるが、その場合は「リスク」などの悪い意味に引っ張られやすいことを意識して、文全体の表現を整えなければならない。（例えば、Chances are growing だと「リスクが大きくなりつつある」と解釈されやすいが、Chances are being created なら「チャンスが生まれている」と解釈されやすい。）

・字面だけを追うと、「の劇的な向上」は「スケーラビリティ」だけにかかるように訳してしまいがちだが、「コスト」「帯域幅」「スケーラビリティ」の三つにかかることが必要。「コストや帯域幅の劇的な向上で機会が生まれる」は自然だが、「コストや帯域幅で機会が生まれる」は不自然、ということから判断できる。日本語では、三つを並べる場合、「AやB、C」とも「A、BやC」とも表現され、英訳時には「読点の位置＝カンマの位置」には必ずしもならない。

(b)

Polar bears depend on sea ice for almost every aspect of their lives, including hunting, traveling, and breeding. NASA satellites have been tracking changes in sea ice, and the data shows that Arctic sea ice shrank at an average rate of about 53,100 km2 over the 1979-2019 period.

＜解答のポイント＞

・「ホッキョクグマ」は polar bears または white bears。north pole bears ならば類推して正しい解釈をすることは可能だが、表現としては不自然。

・bear は、同音の bare と混同しないように注意。

・「海氷」は sea ice または ocean ice。glacier（氷河）や iceberg（氷山）では不適切。

	・「ほぼすべて」と「すべて」は意味が違うため、「ほぼ」は確実に訳すこと。 ・「北極の海氷」は、「北極の」を形容詞としてとらえ、Arctic sea ice とするのが適切。字面を直訳して sea ice of the North Pole とすると、「北極点の海氷」となり不適切。 ・「縮小している」は現在進行形で訳したくなるが、「1979年から2019年」という過去のデータであることに注意。単純過去の shrank で「縮小した」とするか、あるいは過去進行形の was shrinking で「縮小していった」として訳すのが適切。
(c)	A suspension is a liquid containing small solid particles dispersed in it. For example, shaking soil and water in a container results in a suspension. When the suspension is filtered, the solid particles are collected as a residue. When the suspension is left undisturbed, the solid particles slowly settle to the bottom of the container and form a sediment. **＜解答のポイント＞** ・模範解答例では「粒子が回収される」は the particles are collected と表現されているが、collect を自動詞として使い、the particles collect としてもよい。自動詞の collect は「溜まる/積もる」の意でよく使われ、この文脈に合う。 ・「ろ過する」は他動詞の filter で表すのが最も簡潔。filtrate でも良いが、filter の方が一般的。 ・第3文は長めなので、分割を考えること。「ろ過すると」と「放置すると」にそれぞれ when をあてて訳すのが一般的だが、複数の when 節が1文中にあると、係り受けを見極めにくくなる。2文に分けた方が、訳しやすく、ミスをしづらい。その際、2文の文型を揃えるとより読みやすくなる（パラレリズム）。 ・「小さな」はここでは small が合う。他の語でも良いが、次文へのつながりを考慮し、「土」からイメージされる粒子サイズに合わせるべき。例えば、micro なら合わないことはないが、nano では小さすぎる。「専門用語風な響き」で選ぶのではなく、「意味が合っているか」を重視すること。

選択2問各35点

第127回技術英検1級　2021.11　解答

I　(a) 1　(b) 1　(c) 3　(d) 3　(e) 2　　　　　　　　　20 点

II　(a-1) 10 (a-2) 2　(b-1) 5　(b-2) 4　(c-1) 7　(c-2) 11　30 点

III　(a) 3　(b) 3　(c) 1　(d) 2　(e) 1　　　　　　　　30 点

IV　(a) 3　(b) 10　(c) 8　(d) 1　　　　　　　　　　20 点

V

(a)

> 日本の動物相はユーラシア大陸のそれに近い。これは日本列島が大陸とつながっていた氷河期に大陸本土から動物が移動してきたことによる。しかし、屋久島・種子島と奄美大島の動物相の間にはかなり大きな違いがあり、大陸とのつながりと断絶を繰り返した歴史を反映している。歴史的にも地理的にも孤立したこれらの島々には、多くの固有種が生息している。

＜解答のポイント＞
・ユーラシア大陸はヨーロッパとアジアから成る大陸の呼称で、アフリカ大陸とも地続きになっているイメージが出るとよい。
・文章は自然な流れで、過不足なく書かれていることが重要。
問題1文目
・is close to that of は、that of を意識して、「～のそれ（動物相）」を入れて訳す。
問題2文目
・migration は、動物の場合は「移動する、渡る」が自然で、「移住する」のは人。
・during the ice age when は、「氷河期に」でよい。during につられて「氷河期の間に、氷河期の時代の最中に」は冗長。
・connected to the mainland は、「大陸本土とつながる／地続きになる」ということ。「接続する」は日本語として不自然。mainland には島は含まれない。
問題3文目
・significant difference は、「重大な違い、重要な違い」と表現するよりは「かなり大

(a)	きい違い、著しい違い」の方が自然。 ・Yakushima-Tanegashima Islands and Amamioshima Island は、動物相に大きな違いが見られるのは、屋久島・種子島の動物相と奄美大島の動物相の間なので、比較する対象を明確に書くこと。屋久島と種子島は隣接しており、ハイフンは両島を一つのエリアとして表すために用いられている。「屋久島から種子島の諸島」ではない。 ・connections は、問題2文目の connect と同様、「つながる、地続きになる」ということで、「接続する、連結する」はここでは不可。
(b)	ROM は恒久的なデータを収めたコンピュータのメモリチップである。ROM は不揮発性であり、コンピュータの電源を切った後でもデータを保持する。ROM は、コンピュータの電源を入れたときにコンピュータを起動させる基本入出力システム（BIOS）のような、重要なプログラムを保存している。BIOS は数キロバイトのコードで構成され、ハードウェア診断の実行やオペレーティングシステムの RAM への読み込みといった、コンピュータの起動時に行う処理を指示する。 **＜解答のポイント＞** ・ROM や RAM のように、日本語として一般的な言葉になっているものはそのまま使ってよい。 ・カタカナ語は、一般的に通用している場合を除き、なるべく乱用しないようにする。 ・直訳にならないように、過不足なく読みやすい日本語にする。 問題1文目 ・refers to は、「～のことである、～のことを指す、～を言う」という意味。 ・containing permanent data の contain は、「含む」というより「～を収めた、保管した」という意味。permanent data は、「恒久的なデータ、永久的なデータ」という意味。 問題2文目 ・ROM is non-volatile: のコロンは、以降で非揮発性を説明しているものであり、「つまり、すなわち」という意味。その意味が分かるような訳文になっていること。日本文に：をそのまま使うのは不自然。 ・even after は、「～でも」、「～もなお」というニュアンスを入れて訳す。 問題3文目 ・the basic input/output system (BIOS) は、「バイオス」という呼称も一般的だが、ここでは敢えてスペルアウトしているので、「基本入出力システム（BIOS）」と丁寧に訳す。 ・boot up や start up はカタカナよりも「立ち上げる、起動する」が一般的。 問題4文目 ・長文で、such as 以降は that 節にかかっているので、the BIOS consists of a few kilobytes of code を先に訳してから、that 節以降をつなげると日本語として自然な流れになる。

選択1問30点

127

VI

(a)

Welding is a method of joining metal parts by heating them until they melt and pressing them together. Some materials may change in properties or deteriorate when exposed to high heat. Therefore, it is necessary to confirm that the parts have the durability specified by given standards.

＜解答のポイント＞
・第1文は定義文である。この問題文では「溶接とは～方法である」とあるので、Welding is a method の構文を使用する。
・「部材同士を接合する方法」は a method of/for joining metal parts とする。日本語では「部材同士」となっているが、その前に「金属部品」とあり、同一物を指すので metal は必須である。情報の後出し文にしないこと。
・method は process など方法を表す他の語でも置換可能。
・method の後の前置詞は of が普通だが、現在では for も同じように使用されている。method to 不定詞の構文は不可。
・method of/for ～ing O の形は、よく使われるので覚えること。～ing は他動詞の現在分詞形。O は他動詞の目的語が来る。
・「溶けるまで加熱」して「一緒に押さえる」ことで金属部品どうしが接合される。並列要素の前の修飾語は直後の要素のみに係っているのか両方の要素に係っているのかは、文脈と技術的な知識の両方で都度判断しなければならない。
・「接合する」は join がベスト。adhere は不可。adhere は接着する（くっつく）という意味の自動詞。インターネットで調べると他動詞用法が見つかるが真似をしない方がよい。
・「材料によっては」は Some materials とする。Some of the materials は「材料のうち何種類かは」の意味。2つの違いをよく理解して実践に応用すること。
・材料の「性質が変化したり」、「（材料が）劣化したり」という意味。性質は characteristics でも properties でもよいが、特別な例を除いて複数形が自然。
・「恐れがある」は助動詞の may で表現する。
・「溶接を行う際は」は「溶接の前に」と読み替えると論理的になる。ここでは、懸垂分詞構文を避けること。

(b)

In general, the steel used in reinforced concrete has already been exposed to water and to oxygen in the air. As a result, such steel is usually partially corroded, covered with a layer of iron oxide. Once the steel is inside the hardened concrete, however, it will be protected from air and water, and thus prevented from further oxidization.

(b)	**＜解答のポイント＞** ・第1文の「事前に～さらされている」を字句通りによると「前もってさらされている」となるが、自然にさらされた状態になっていることである。「既に」のイメージ。したがってこの部分は完了形でなければならない。 ・「鋼」は steel。鉄 (iron)、metal とは定義が異なる。 ・「鉄筋コンクリート」は reinforced concrete（頭字語：RC）あるいは armored concrete が一般的。 ・第3文の意味を解釈する。「鋼は硬化したコンクリートの内部では」とするのが最も簡潔だが、「鋼は硬化したコンクリートの内部にあると」とすれば解決する。つまり問題文の「いったん」は冗長な不要語で、「内部に入ると」は不適切な表現である。人の書いた文を読むときはこのように不適切な部分を是正できる能力を持つ必要がある。「鋼はいったん硬化したコンクリートの内部に埋め込まれると (embedded)」でもよい。 ・「～に使用される」は used in。用途を表す前置詞は for でなく in が正しい。 ・「さらなる酸化」は further oxidation。
(c)	Frequency is the number of waves that pass a fixed point per unit time, or the number of cycles or vibrations per unit time that a body in periodic motion undergoes. The most common unit of frequency is the hertz; 1 Hz is equal to one cycle per second. **＜解答のポイント＞** ・技術用語を正しく使用できるかどうかを問う問題。第1文は定義文である。 ・「波の数」は the number of waves とする。不定冠詞で a number of waves とすると「多くの波」あるいは「いくつかの波」の意味になるので注意が必要。 ・「単位時間内にある」は per unit time とする。per のうしろは単数無冠詞の名詞が続く。「毎秒」は per second。 ・「物体」は object がベスト。UFO は undefined flying object（未確認飛行物体）の略である。この語を覚えておくと応用が利く。 ・「周期または振動の数」は「波の数」の応用で the number of cycles or vibrations とする。ここは係り受けを間違わないこと。 ・振動数の「1ヘルツ」をスペルアウトするときは one hertz だが、記号を使用するときは1 Hz となる。できるだけ後者を使用すること。

選択2問各35点

第126回技術英検1級　2021.6　解答

Ⅰ　(a) 1　(b) 3　(c) 2　(d) 2　(e) 1　　　　　　　　　20点

Ⅱ　(a-1) 6　(a-2) 8　(b-1) 1　(b-2) 11　(c-1) 12　(c-2) 3　30点

Ⅲ　(a) 2　(b) 2　(c) 3　(d) 1　(e) 3　　　　　　　　30点

Ⅳ　(a) 10　(b) 4　(c) 9　(d) 1　　　　　　　　　　　20点

Ⅴ

(a)

ハイドロフォーミング（液圧成形）は、アルミニウムや超軽量鋼などの材料を成形する方法である。金属を、液圧を用いて型に押し込む方法だ。たとえば、車体用の部品を製造するには、鋼管を金型内に配置して高圧をかけ押し込むことで、金属をまさに必要とされる形状にすることができる。このように部品をハイドロフォーミングすると、スタンピング（打ち抜き加工）や溶接などのいくつかの異なる操作が不要になる。ハイドロフォーミングは、より軽量で高い強度が求められる場合に利用される。

＜解答のポイント＞
・ハイドロフォーミングは金型の中に金属を置いて、液圧をかけて金型にぴったりと合うようにする成型法であることを念頭に入れて訳す。
・スチール、スチールチューブ、モールド、ウェルディングといったカタカナは、相手に意味が正確に伝わらない場合もあるので、特に指定が無い限り、「鋼、鉄鋼」「鋼管」「金型」「溶接」と一般的に使われている言葉で書く。
問題1文目
・ultralight steel は「超軽量鋼」。steel は「鉄」「金属」ではない。
問題2文目
・is pushed into shape は、「型に押し込む」ことであり、「押し出す」のではない。
問題3文目
・車体用の部品の製造工程は、時系列に従って書くと読みやすくなる。

(a)	鋼管を金型内に配置→高圧をかけ押し込む→目的の形状にする ・exact shape required は「まさに必要とされる形状」「必要とされる形状通りに」など、exact の意味が出るように訳出すること。 問題5文目 ・high strength の strength は「強度」。剛性（外からの力に対する物体の変形のしにくさ）とは異なる。
(b)	医学生が手術の練習をする安価な手段はほとんどない。バーチャルリアリティ（VR）によるシミュレータは役に立つが、まだひとつ問題がある。それは、学生たちが効果的な方法で実際の環境に触れられないということだ。ある会社が、この問題を解決するため、新しい VR 手術シミュレータを開発した。触覚（*注）フィードバックを組み込み、医者が実際の手術と同様に動きを「感じる」ことができるようにした。この新しいシミュレータはわずか8,000ドルで、これまでのシステムよりはるかに安価だ。 *注：検定時、本問題の脚注に誤りがありました。お詫びして訂正いたします。 【誤】haptic：触角の　【正】haptic：触覚の 「触角フィードバック」「触覚フィードバック」いずれも、採点対象にしておりません。 **＜解答のポイント＞** ・センテンスごとに主語が変わるが、それぞれ主語を明確にしながら訳すこと。 問題1文目 ・この文脈では、不定冠詞の a を伴わない few は「ほとんどない」という意味で、「少ない」「多くない」ではない。 ・affordable ways は、「安価な手段」「手頃な手段」であり、「許容できる／された手段」「適当な手段」ではない。 問題2文目 ・Virtual-reality (VR) simulators will help の will は強い意志を表しているので、「役立つ」と言い切る。 「かもしれない」「～と思われている」ではない。 ・students cannot touch the actual environment とは、学生が効果的（有意義な）方法で実際（に手術しているとき）の環境に触れることができない（感触を得られない）ということ。 問題4文目 ・can "feel" their actions は、医者が実際に手術をしているかのような「動きを感じることができる」ということ 問題5文目 ・as little as（わずか、たった）、far less than（はるかに安価）といった数量表現は正確に訳すこと。

選択1問30点

VI

(a)

This vacuum cleaner is designed to give you many years of excellent performance. If regularly serviced, it will cost you less in the long run. We offer a free repair assessment by our service engineers on our products out of warranty.

＜解答のポイント＞

問題1文目
・「掃除機」は vacuum cleaner または cleaner のみでもよい。vacuum machine（真空パック機）など、類似の語と混同しないように注意。
・「長年」は重要情報。「長く使えるように作ってあるので、定期点検を受けながら使うとお得です」という、2文目へのつながりを意識して丁寧に訳すこと。

問題2文目
・「コストパフォーマンス」は解答例のような表現の他、形容詞の cost-effective を使った表現がわかりやすい。
・「定期点検」は、文脈から「保守」が目的であることが明らかなので、service や maintenance を使うのがよい。

問題3文目
・「修理査定」は「修理にかかる費用を査定する」ということ。offer を使うことで「（保証対象外の製品は、修理は有料だが）費用の査定は無料です（のでまずはご連絡ください）。」というニュアンスになる。
・この文脈での「保証」は「修理保証」なので warranty。guarantee や assurance との違いに注意。
・費用に関する文脈では、重要情報の訳抜けがないように、特に意識すること。

(b)

Plate tectonics is a theory explaining the movement of the rock layers that form the earth's surface. The theory, formulated in the 1960s, significantly changed earth sciences by providing a uniform context for understanding mountain-building processes, volcanoes, earthquakes, and the evolution of the earth's surface.

＜解答のポイント＞

問題1文目
・時制は現在。
・plate tectonics は s で終わっているが単数扱い。the は不要。physics や mathematics と同様。
・explaining は that explains でもよい。
・the movement（中略）the earth's surface は、how the rock layers that form the earth's surface move でもよい。
・この文脈での rock は不可算がよい。複数の岩がごろごろ転がっているイメージではなく「岩という材質でできた層」のイメージになる。
・earth は先頭大文字でもよい。

	問題2文目 ・時制は過去。 ・The theory, formulated in the 1960s, … の２つのカンマは、なくても意味は通じるが、あった方が読みやすい。 ・「造山の過程や火山、地震や地球の表面の進化」のように多くの項目がリストされている部分は、区切りが明確になるように訳すこと。「造山の過程」「火山」「地震」「地球の表面の進化」と区切るのが正しいが、漫然と訳すと他の区切り方もできる英語になりやすい。例えば、the processes of mountain building, volcanoes, earthquakes, and the evolution of the earth's surface としても間違いではないのだが、「『造山や火山や地震や地球の表面の進化』の過程」とも解釈できてしまい、読みづらくなる。
(c)	A colloid is a substance that is not dissolved or suspended but is dispersed in a liquid. A colloid consists of particles that are larger than atoms or ordinary molecules but too small to be visible to the naked eye. Examples of colloids include milk, starch, and ink. **＜解答のポイント＞** 問題1文目 ・「コロイドとは何か」を定義する文なので、「コロイド」を主語にするのがよい。 ・「懸濁」を表す suspend は他動詞しかないので、「コロイド」を主語にすると必然的に受動態になる（文法的に能動態は作れない）。dissolve と disperse は自動詞他動詞のいずれでも使えるが、suspend と用法をそろえた方が読みやすい。したがって、３つの動詞すべてを受動態で使うことになる。 問題2文目 ・意味に注意して、文の区切りを捉えること。「原子や通常の分子よりも大きい」は「肉眼で見るには小さすぎる」と並列で、共に「粒子」を修飾しているので、そのように訳す必要がある。「コロイドは粒子で構成されている。その粒子のサイズはこのぐらいだ」というように頭の中を整理し、関係代名詞を使えば、正しい英文が作りやすい。「コロイドは、原子や通常の分子よりも大きい」と「肉眼で見るには小さすぎる粒子で構成されている」の２文を訳して and でつなぎがちだが、それでは意味が異なる。 ・too small to be visible to the naked eye は、too small to see with the naked eye でもよい。so small that they are invisible to the naked eye も可。 ・consists of は is composed of でもよい。composes や composes of は不可。 問題3文目 ・include は、are でもよい。 ・「など」は冗長表現なので、訳出しなくてよい（Examples にその意味が含まれている）

選択2問各 35 点

第 125 回技術英検 1 級　2021. 1　解答

I　(a) 3　(b) 2　(c) 1　(d) 2　(e) 3　　　　　　　　　　20 点

II　(a-1) 6　(a-2) 12 (b-1) 4　(b-2) 5　(c-1) 10 (c-2) 7　30 点

III　(a) 2　(b) 3　(c) 2　(d) 3　(e) 2　　　　　　　　　30 点

IV　(a) 5　(b) 4　(c) 9　(d) 7　　　　　　　　　　　　20 点

V

(a)

ニュートンの運動の第 3 法則である作用・反作用の法則とは、物体に力が加わるとき、等しい大きさの力が同時に反対方向に働くことをいう。簡単に言うと、何かが物体を押した時、その物体は等しい力で押し返している。車にエンジンがかかり、車輪を回転させた時、車輪は道路を押し、道路はその反対の力で押し返すことで車を前進させている。

＜解答のポイント＞

解答 1 文目
・キーワードであるニュートンの「運動の第 3 法則」、「作用・反作用の法則」を正しく和訳できていること。
・a force acts upon an object の upon は、「物体に力がかかる」ことで、「上に、上から」という位置関係を示しているのではない。
・an equal and opposite force is applied at the same time は、「等しい大きさの力が同時に反対方向に働く」という意味。opposite force は「反対向きの力」であり、「反対側の力」、「反対からの力」ではない。
解答 3 文目
・wheels push against the road の road は「道路、路面」のことで、「地面」ではない。
・the opposing force は、単に「反対の力」ではなく、「その（押した力と同じ大きさの）反対の力」のことである。

134

<table>
<tr><td rowspan="2">(b)</td><td>pH という用語は、水素イオンと水酸化物イオンの濃度を示す0から14の数値である。数値が7における両方のイオンの濃度は等しく、溶液は中性だ。数値が7未満では、液体は酸性で、pH 値が7から0に下がるにつれて水素イオン濃度は上昇する。7を超える場合は、液体はアルカリ性で、pH 値が上昇するにつれて水酸化物イオン濃度は増加する。</td></tr>
<tr><td><解答のポイント>
pH という用語の説明なので、イオン濃度ではなく pH を中心に話を展開させる。
解答3、4文目
・below 7 は「7以下」ではなく、「7未満」、「7を下回る」という意味。同様に、above 7 も「7以上」ではなく「7を上回る」という意味である。
・with… increasing as… falls は、「〜に下がるにつれて〜が増加する」、with… increasing as… increases は、「〜が上昇するにつれて〜が増加する」という意味である。
・alkaline は「アルカリ（性）の」という形容詞で、塩基性の形容詞形は basic である。</td></tr>
</table>

選択1問30点

VI

<table>
<tr><td rowspan="2">(a)</td><td>The sun produces a solar wind that contains charged particles such as electrons and protons. These particles escape the sun's intense gravity because of their high kinetic energy and the high temperature of the sun's corona, an atmospheric-pressure plasma that extends into space.</td></tr>
<tr><td><解答のポイント>
問題1文目
・a. 太陽が太陽風を作り出す (The sun creates a solar wind)
　b. 太陽風には荷電粒子が含まれる (a solar wind contains charged particles)
　c. 荷電粒子には電子や陽子などがある (electrons and protons are charged particles)
　上記 a, b, c の関係性が崩れないように英訳することが大事である。
・「作り出す」は、creates/generates でもよい。
問題2文目
・2文目は長いため、文を分けずに訳す場合、説明の係り受けが離れるとわかりづらくなるため、注意する。
具体的には、
a. 荷電粒子 (charged particles) が太陽の重力から解かれる (escape the gravity)
b. 太陽風コロナ (solar corona) とその説明 (atmospheric pressure plasma…)
の2つを近づけることが大事である。
・「重力から解き放たれる」は、escape from the gravity が最も一般的な訳である。</td></tr>
</table>

135

・「強い重力」は、strong gravity でも良い。heavy, big, huge は適切ではない。
・「運動エネルギー」=「kinetic energy」【mechanical energy/ motion energy(力学的エネルギー)は運動エネルギーと位置エネルギーの和を指す】
・「の一種である」は、a type of や a kind of としてもよい。
・「atmospheric pressure plasma」は「normal pressure plasma」でもよい。
・「宇宙」はこの場合、太陽系内の宇宙空間を指すため、「universe」より「space」または「outer space」が適切である。
「space/ outer space」は「the」はつかない。
・「宇宙に広がる」は、expands toward space としてもよい。

(b)

The Metropolitan Area Outer Underground Discharge Channel, known for the G-Cans Project, is a concrete underground channel system running 50 meters deep and 6.5 kilometers long. This huge structure was built in the 14 years from 1992 to 2006. About seven times a year, it diverts water from heavy rainstorms and keeps the streets of Tokyo from turning into raging rivers.

< 解答のポイント >

問題1文目
・解答例「concrete underground channel system」のように、concrete を先に持ってくる構文を使うと、短い文章で書くことができる。
・concrete を underground channel system の後ろに持ってくる場合、made of が必要になり、underground channel system made of concrete となる。
・run は「ある方向に向かっている様」を示す動詞で、第2文型の be 動詞の代わりとして使われる。
例：The tunnel is 20-meter long = The tunnel runs 20-meter long
・「concrete underground channel system running 50 meters deep and 6.5 kilometers long.」は「concrete-made, 50-meter-deep, and 6.5-kilometer-long underground channel system.」としてもよい。
・深さ、長さを表すのに、…deep/…long の他、…in depth/…in length としてもよい。
　構文によっては、have 動詞を取り、has a depth of… / a length of… としてもよい。
問題2文目
・It took 14 years, from 1992 to 2006, to build this huge structure. としてもよい。
問題3文目
・「迂回させる」は、reroute としてもよい。
・「防いでいる」は、keep または prevent を使う場合「keep (prevent) X from ＋動名詞」の構文を取る必要がある。

(c)

Mammals are warm-blooded animals that have skin covered with hair. In general, female mammals give birth to babies rather than laying eggs, and feed their young with milk secreted from their own body. Some mammals including whales and seals live in the sea, whereas others including horses, monkeys, and humans live on land.

＜解答のポイント＞

問題1文目
・「哺乳類とは」という説明文なので、主役となる mammals を主語として始めるのが望ましい。
・関係代名詞所有格 whose を使った構文で Mammals are warm-blooded animals whose skins are covered with hair. としてもよい。

問題2文目
・「子供を産む」は、give birth を使う場合、前置詞 to を忘れないこと。deliver/ bear でもよい。
注意すべき点は、baby は動物と人間で共通して使えるが、child, children は人間の子供のみにしか使えず、人間も含めた動物には the young、または the youngling を使う必要がある。

問題3文目
・「海に住んでいるが、馬、…」は、1節目と2節目で反対のことを述べているわけではないので、接続詞は but ではなく、日本語で「～である一方で」に相当する whereas/ while などの語を使うのがよい。
・「などの」は including のほかに such as としてもよい。

選択2問各35点

第124回技術英検１級　2020.11　解答

Ⅰ　(a) 2　　(b) 1　　(c) 3　　(d) 3　　(e) 1　　　　　　　20点

Ⅱ　(a-1) 6　(a-2) 3　(b-1) 5　(b-2) 10 (c-1) 4　(c-2) 11　30点

Ⅲ　(a) 3　　(b) 2　　(c) 1　　(d) 2　　(e) 1　　　　　　　30点

Ⅳ　(a) 11　(b) 9　　(c) 8　　(d) 1　　　　　　　　　　　20点

Ⅴ

<table>
<tr><td></td><td>目は、虹彩の中にメラニンと呼ばれる天然の化学物質を含んでいる。メラニンが多いほど、目の色は濃くなる。目の色が実際の物の見え方に違いをもたらすかもしれないと考えた人もいる。実のところ、目の色は見え方に影響することはないが、照明の条件による視力の違いを引き起こすことがある。虹彩細胞の色素中のメラニン濃度が高いことは、虹彩を強力な日光から守る作用もある。</td></tr>
<tr><td>(a)</td><td><解答のポイント>
極端に直訳にならないように、過不足のない自然な日本語になっていることが望ましい。
・a natural chemical は「天然の化学物質」であり、「自然化学物質」、「自然な〜」は減点の対象となる。
・the more…the darker the color will be は比較級の対比を明確に示していること。darker は目の色のことなので、暗いというよりは濃い、または黒いが適切。
ここの will は未来形ではなく強い意志を表している。「〜だろう」ではなく断定すること。
・may make a difference to は推量の may として「〜かもしれない」、</td></tr>
</table>

(a)	「〜の可能性がある」と訳す。 ・while eye color does not affect how people see something, it can cause them to have… は、文章が「〜はないが、〜ことがある」という流れになっていること。can は可能性の can であることを明確にすること。 ・lighting conditions は「光の当たり方」、「照明の条件」のニュアンスであり、単に「光」や「日照」ではない。 ・the melanin concentration は、文脈から判断すると、「メラニンの濃度が高い、メラニンが集中している」というニュアンスになる。
(b)	再充電可能なリチウム金属電池を開発するという試みは、安全上の問題で失敗に終わった。特に充電中に見られるリチウム金属固有の不安定さのため、研究の対象はリチウムイオンを使用した非金属リチウム電池へ移行した。リチウムイオン電池は、リチウム金属電池よりもエネルギー密度がわずかに低いが、充放電の際に一定の対策を講じれば安全である。リチウムイオンのエネルギー密度は、標準的なニッケルカドミウムのエネルギー密度の2倍程度だが、さらに高いエネルギー密度を得られる可能性がある。 ＜解答のポイント＞ 製品の技術的な説明文である。 ・rechargeable lithium-metal batteries の rechargeable は「再充電可能な、充電可能な」という意味。「二次電池」も可。 ・the inherent instability of lithium metal の inherent は「固有の、〜に内在する」という意味。本来そういう性質を持っているというニュアンスを訳出する。 ・…are safe, provided that certain precautions are taken は「一定の対策を講じれば安全である」という条件付きであることを訳出する。take a precaution とは「きちんと注意すべきこと」というニュアンスとなる。 ・typically twice that of は「2倍程度、通常2倍」という意味。 ・have potential for は「〜の可能性がある」という意味。

選択1問30点

Ⅵ

<table>
<tr>
<td rowspan="2">(a)</td>
<td>Transportation is the largest source of greenhouse-gas emissions in the US and fourth largest globally. Therefore, major shifts to cleaner vehicles and mass transit systems are essential; there is no other way to achieve the reductions necessary to avoid dangerous levels of global warming.</td>
</tr>
<tr>
<td>

<解答のポイント>

・「～の排出源」と「～の達成」の2フレーズは修飾語が多数あるので、直訳すると修飾・被修飾の関係が誤った状態になりやすい。訳した後の英文が、「運輸活動は米国最大であり、『世界で4番目の温室効果ガス』の排出源である」「『地球温暖化を回避するために必要な排出』の削減」といった誤った係り受けになってしまっていないか、前置詞句や関係代名詞節の位置や順番を丁寧に見直すことが必要。

・正確に訳すには、「似て非なる語」を訳語に充てないことも重要。例えば「排出」を exhaust と訳してしまう例が見られるが、exhaust は「排気」すなわち「機械や工場から出る使用済み・燃焼済み気体」であり、「温室効果ガスの『排出』」の意味には使えない。
</td>
</tr>
<tr>
<td rowspan="2">(b)</td>
<td>Mass, in physics, is a quantitative measure of inertia and is a fundamental property of all matter. It is the resistance that a body offers to a change in its speed or position upon the application of a force. The greater the mass of a body, the smaller the change produced by an applied force.</td>
</tr>
<tr>
<td>

<解答のポイント>

・「質量」は mass と訳すこと。weight や amount とは概念が異なる。

・「物質」は、物理的な特徴（質量・重量・速度・慣性等）を表した文脈では matter が合う。substance は物質の種類や化学的な特徴を表した文脈に合う用語であり、ここでは不適。

・「物体」は body または object が用語としては一般的。thing も可。
</td>
</tr>
</table>

(c)

All weather changes result from temperature changes in different parts of the atmosphere. Our lives and weather depend on the sun's energy radiated to the earth. On the earth, the areas near the equator receive more heat from the sun than those near the North and South Poles. This unequal heating of the earth causes north and south winds.

＜解答のポイント＞

・「気象／天候」は weather あるいは meteorological conditions。climate は「気候」であり、概念が異なる。

・簡潔な表現を心がけるあまり、意味が変わってしまわないように気を付けること。例えば、「北極や南極に近い地域」は the areas near the North and South Poles だが、簡潔に the Arctic および the Antarctic で表すのは良い。しかし、the North and South Poles のみでは、「近い地域」ではなく「北極点と南極点」を表してしまうので不可となる。

選択2問各35点

第122回工業英検準2級　2020.1　解答

Ⅰ　(a) 2　　(b) 1　　(c) 3　　(d) 2　　(e) 1　　　　　　　　　20点

Ⅱ　(a-1) 7　(a-2) 1　(b-1) 9　(b-2) 8　(c-1) 12　(c-2) 5　　30点

Ⅲ　(a) 3　　(b) 2　　(c) 3　　(d) 1　　(e) 1　　　　　　　　　30点

Ⅳ　(a) 7　　(b) 10　　(c) 4　　(d) 9　　　　　　　　　　　　　20点

Ⅴ

(a)	メタンハイドレートは、メタン分子1個が、インターロックした水分子のカゴに囲まれている結晶性固体である。
(b)	人間もそうだが、生物の体内には生物学的な時計があり、一日の規則的なリズムに前もって備えたり、それに順応したりすることを助けている。
(c)	摩擦とは、二つの表面が互いに接触してずれ動くときに生じる抵抗の力である。摩擦抵抗は、摩擦係数として測定される。
(d)	極端に高温または低温の場所や直射日光のあたる場所では、本装置を使用しないでください。

30点

Ⅵ

(a)	(1)	タービンはシャフトによって、エアフィルターと吸気マニホールドの間にあるコンプレッサーにつながっている。
	(2)	シリンダーからの排気がタービンの羽根の間を通り、これによってタービンが回転する。
(b)	(1)	例えば、カンガルーは進化系統が比較的新しく、遺伝学的に似通っている。
	(2)	より遺伝学的に多様な分類群を保護することに注力すべきだと考える科学者もいる。

40 点

Ⅶ

(a)	This discovery led to the development of new drugs, which offer hope to patients with advanced cancer which was previously untreatable.
(b)	Some wavelengths of light are long while others are short. Light of different wavelengths appears as different colors.
(c)	The substances that go into a chemical reaction are called reactants, and the substances produced at the end of the reaction are called products.

30 点

第121回工業英検準2級　2019.11　解答

Ⅰ　(a) 2　　(b) 3　　(c) 1　　(d) 3　　(e) 1　　　　　　　　　20点

Ⅱ　(a-1) 6　(a-2) 8　(b-1) 9　(b-2) 3　(c-1) 11　(c-2) 10　30点

Ⅲ　(a) 3　　(b) 1　　(c) 1　　(d) 1　　(e) 2　　　　　　　　30点

Ⅳ　(a) 6　　(b) 11　　(c) 4　　(d) 8　　　　　　　　　　　　20点

Ⅴ

(a)	これらのブール演算子を用いると返ってくるデータの量を大きく減らすあるいは増加させることができる。
(b)	伝導により、熱は素材全体に伝わり、場合によってはその熱い素材と接触している他の素材にも伝わる。
(c)	有機分子において最も一般的な結合は、2つの原子間で電子を共有する共有結合である。
(d)	液体の粘度は温度の上昇に伴い減少するが、空気の粘度は温度とともに増加する。

30点

VI

(a)	(1)	鼓膜が振動すると、脳はその振動を音と解釈する。これが音が聞こえる原理である。
	(2)	鼓膜を振動させる原因で最も一般的なのは、気圧の素早い変動だ。
(b)	(1)	人工知能とロボット工学の発達により、複数のドローンを同時に動かすことが可能になるだろう。
	(2)	輸送会社の中には、パイロットなしで人を運ぶ、空飛ぶタクシーのようなヘリコプターサイズのドローンを設計しているところもある。

40点

VII

(a)	Recent studies have revealed that zooplankton eat microplastics, taking them for phytoplankton.
(b)	Even when the car is simply idling by the roadside, the piston still needs to move up and down roughly 1,000 times per minute.
(c)	Soap making requires careful measurements because some ingredients are potentially hazardous.

30点

第 120 回工業英検準 2 級　2019.7　解答

Ⅰ　(a) 2　(b) 1　(c) 3　(d) 1　(e) 3　　　　　　　　20 点

Ⅱ　(a-1) 7　(a-2) 1　(b-1) 10　(b-2) 4　(c-1) 9　(c-2) 6　30 点

Ⅲ　(a) 2　(b) 1　(c) 1　(d) 3　(e) 3　　　　　　　　30 点

Ⅳ　(a) 6　(b) 8　(c) 11　(d) 2　　　　　　　　　　　20 点

Ⅴ

(a)	機械加工とは、機械を用いて、被加工材（ワークピースという）を切削し、部品に成形することである。
(b)	たんぱく質と結合した薬物分子は、たんぱく質分子が大きすぎて毛細血管の窓を通り抜けることができないため、各組織まで到達できない。
(c)	二酸化炭素濃度が増加すると、海水の酸性化が進み、海洋生物を絶滅の危険にさらすおそれがある。
(d)	センサー技術や AI 技術の発達により、サービスロボットはますます身近なものとなった。今やわれわれは、ロボットをペットやコミュニケーションの相手として利用している。

30 点

VI

(a)	(1)	油圧ブレーキ回路には、フルードで満たされたマスターシリンダーとスレーブシリンダーがあり、これらは導管でつながっている。
	(2)	ブレーキペダルを踏むと、マスターシリンダー内のピストンが押し込まれ、押し出されたフルードが導管を伝って流れていく。
(b)	(1)	宇宙服の外層は、テフロン加工のグラスファイバー生地で出来ており、微小隕石に対する防護に役立っている。
	(2)	ヘルメットにはバイザーが装備されていて、宇宙飛行士の目を紫外線放射から防護している。

40点

VII

(a)	Therefore, if a is greater than b, the object receives a force W greater than the applied force F.
(b)	The most familiar compound, or combination, of sodium and another element is common salt.
(c)	Such precautions reduce the risk of accidental activation of power tools.

30点

第119回工業英検準2級　2019.5　解答

Ⅰ　(a) 3　(b) 2　(c) 3　(d) 1　(e) 2　　　　　　　　20点

Ⅱ　(a-1) 5　(a-2) 11　(b-1) 8　(b-2) 10　(c-1) 4　(c-2) 3　30点

Ⅲ　(a) 1　(b) 2　(c) 1　(d) 3　(e) 3　　　　　　　　30点

Ⅳ　(a) 5　(b) 8　(c) 3　(d) 11　　　　　　　　　　20点

Ⅴ

(a)	燃料電池は蓄電池と異なり、一定期間ごとに充電する必要がなく、燃料が供給される限り電気を生成し続ける。
(b)	細胞は人体の構造を作り、栄養を取り込み、これらの栄養をエネルギーに変換し、特殊な働きを行う。
(c)	電気工学は比較的大きな電流を扱うのに対し、電子工学はわずかな電流を用いて物を制御する方法を扱う。
(d)	重力波が出現して11時間足らずで、天文学者たちは、天空に新しい可視光の点を見つけた。

30点

Ⅵ

(a)	(1)	データは、アナログの信号の形式でも送れるし、デジタルのビットストリームに変換することもできる。
	(2)	データは、ネットワークを使わずに送ることもできる。例えば、メモリーデバイスにコピーして別の場所に運ぶこともできる。
(b)	(1)	風は、この低気圧の目と地球の自転によって引き起こされる。
	(2)	熱帯低気圧は、北半球では反時計回りに、南半球では時計回りに回転する。

40 点

Ⅶ

(a)	The balance is a part that consists of a balance wheel and a balance spring, and plays an important role in keeping the time accurately.
(b)	· With our lives becoming/going/moving more and more online, monitoring by the authorities can have a devastating impact on our privacy rights. · As our lives become/go/move more and more online, our privacy rights can be seriously affected by those in power.
(c)	Most food chains are based on sunlight, which plays an important role in photosynthesis and allows plants to grow.

30 点

第118回工業英検準2級　2019.1　解答

Ⅰ　(a) 2　(b) 3　(c) 2　(d) 1　(e) 1　　　　　　　20点

Ⅱ　(a-1) 2　(a-2) 11　(b-1) 8　(b-2) 9　(c-1) 12　(c-2) 7　　30点

Ⅲ　(a) 1　(b) 3　(c) 2　(d) 1　(e) 3　　　　　　　30点

Ⅳ　(a) 4　(b) 5　(c) 11　(d) 7　　　　　　　　　20点

Ⅴ

(a)	現在手に入る遺伝子組み換え作物には、害虫に強い遺伝子を持つものがあるが、近年はより栄養価の高いものも研究されている。
(b)	歩行ロボットを設計する際の重要な要素のひとつは、特定の歩行パターンに対応する足の動きの順序を制御することである。
(c)	トランジスタのベースとエミッタ間に電圧を加えると、コレクタとエミッタ間に電流を流すことができる。
(d)	当社の新チップは、従来のコンピュータチップの製造に用いられていたのと同じ半導体製造設備、同じ標準材料、また類似の技術を用いて、製造することができる。

30点

VI

(a)	(1)	火山地形は、繰り返される火山活動の結果、時間をかけて徐々に出来てきたものだ。
	(2)	灰と溶岩の層でできた印象的な急斜面を持つ富士山は、典型的な成層火山である。
(b)	(1)	空中に浮遊している汚染物質を空気から取り除くことが不可能であるか、あるいは経済的ではない場合には、必ず呼吸用保護マスクを使用しなければならない。
	(2)	呼吸用マスク内側の顔に接する領域へは、顔面シールが破れない限り、外側から触れることはできない。

40点

VII

(a)	The traditional telephone is an analog device designed to transmit various human voices and tones.
(b)	The larger the magnitude of the earthquake, the more likely the earthquake induces landslides.
(c)	The whole body acts as a pump for sending blood throughout the body, which corresponds to the function of the human heart.

30点

2024 年度版技術英検 1 級問題集

2024 年 3 月 5 日 初版 第 1 刷発行

編著者—一般社団法人日本能率協会　JSTC 技術英語委員会
　　　　©2024 Japan Society for Technical Communication
発行者—張 士洛
発行所—日本能率協会マネジメントセンター
〒 103-6009　東京都中央区日本橋 2-7-1　東京日本橋タワー
TEL 03（6362）4339（編集）／ 03（6362）4558（販売）
FAX 03（3272）8127（編集・販売）
https://www.jmam.co.jp/

装　丁—冨澤崇（EBranch）
印刷所・製本所—三松堂株式会社

ISBN978-4-8005-9171-5 C3082
落丁・乱丁はおとりかえします。
PRINTED IN JAPAN

図面の読み方が
やさしくわかる本

西村 仁 著

技術者以外の方々が「図面を読む」方法を習得するための、やさしい入門書です。商談の場でお客様から図面を提示された時に、瞬時に実際物をイメージできれば、ビジネスの大きな強みとなります。
本書では、そのために必要な「なぜ」の部分(なぜ、その表記なのか、なぜ、この記号なのか……)を基本から丁寧に解説するので、「知識」と共に「思想・考え方」まで、しっかり身につきます。

●A5判　208頁

日本能率協会マネジメントセンター

 **JMAM** の本

図面の描き方が
やさしくわかる本

西村 仁 著

設計製図の知識と技能をキソのキソから知りたい人のための、「図面のルール・JIS製図規格」と「図面を描くコツ」がやさしくわかり、身につく本です。内容は実務で役立つことに重点を置き、よく使う規格はボリュームをとって解説し、そうでないものはおもいきって省略してあります。
図面を「正しく」「明確に」「速く描く」ために、設計製図に関わる人が1冊持っておきたい本です。

●A5判　264頁

日本能率協会マネジメントセンター

これなら通じる
技術英語ライティングの基本

平野 信輔 著

本書は、工業・技術分野の情報を発信するときに必要となる、「正確」「明確」「簡潔」な英文を作成するための初歩的なポイントを解説する本です。解説の形式も先生と生徒の対話形式ですので、堅苦しくなく一人でも読み進めやすい、また間違えやすいポイントがわかりやすい内容となっています。英語の表記法であるパンクチュエーションの説明やミニコラムも充実しており、初学者にぴったりの一冊です。

●A5判　216頁

日本能率協会マネジメントセンター

速効!
英文ライティング

福田 尚代 著

本書は、「明確」「簡潔」「正確」な英文を書くことを目的にルール化された テクニカルライティング(技術英語)のノウハウを使い、主語と動詞の組み 合わせでシンプルな英文を書く技術を身につけることを目的にしています。 このコツをつかむと、あなたの「英語で書く力」は大幅にアップします。 仕事でちょっとした英文を書く必要に迫られた方々、知的でシンプルな英文 を操りたいと考えている方々に向けて、テクニカルライティングのプロ講師 が優しく解説します。

●四六判　232頁

日本能率協会マネジメントセンター

技術系英語
プレゼンテーション教本

川合　ゆみ子 著

プレゼンテーションは「スピーチ」「スライド」「発表スキル」の3つの要素
で完成します。本書はプレゼンの「計画」から「発表」までの流れに沿って、
スピーチ原稿の書き方、スライドの作り方、効果的な話し方や見せ方を豊
富なサンプルで具体的に紹介します。工業英検が提唱する3C(Correct・
Clear・Concise)の実践法を直感的に学べる1冊です。

●A5判　307頁

日本能率協会マネジメントセンター

貿易実務英語の基礎

日本貿易実務検定協会® 編

「貿易実務検定」では、貿易実務における幅広い英語力が求められ、初級のC級では取引交渉時の基本的表現や貿易書類、ビジネス・レターに関する「読み」「書き」の基礎力が必要となります。

本書は、貿易実務検定C級試験過去問ベースの例文で英語力を養成する基礎編とビジネス・レターや貿易用語をまとめた応用編からなり、合格のための英語力が身につく構成となっています。

●四六判　232頁

日本能率協会マネジメントセンター

技術系英文
ライティング教本

中山 裕木子 著

ベストセラーの著者が技術系英文に的を絞り、3Cすなわち正確・明確・簡
潔という工業英語の基本的観点から英文法を解説しました。
各種技術文書への応用までを視野に入れ、ライティングのテクニックを体系
的にまとめた好著です。

●A5判 304頁

日本能率協会マネジメントセンター